The Military Guide to Financial Independence & Retirement

The Military Financial Independence and Retirement Pocket Guide

Doug Nordman

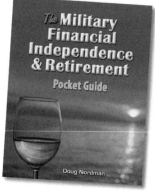

Here's the companion guide for the ground-breaking *Military Guide to Financial Independence and Retirement*. This powerful little pocket guide has it all. It provides servicemembers, veterans, and their families with an important roadmap for becoming financially independent prior to committing themselves to full-time retirement.

Semi-retired at age 41 and enjoying life with his family on the beaches of Hawaii, the author outlines how military personnel who want to retire as early as in their 40s can become happily semi-retired and thus avoid the necessity of pursuing what is often a less than fulfilling second career in government or the corporate world.

Emphasizing the importance of family, lifestyle, and bridge careers, this pocket guide goes a long way in providing answers to one of today's most important questions for transitioning military personnel and their families – *"What do you want to do with the rest of your life?"*

Dispelling numerous myths about military transition, finances, and retirement, the book focuses on the two most important inflation-protected benefits military retirees receive and can build upon for creating a financially independent and semi-retired lifestyle:

- military pension
- TRICARE

It shows how to build a sound financial house based upon:

- military benefits
- savings
- investment portfolios
- bridge careers
- part-time work
- frugal living

Filled with examples, checklists, and recommended websites and books, this guide is essential reading for anyone contemplating retiring from the military or jump-starting their post-military career in the direction of semi-retirement and/or full-time retirement.

64 pages. 3 $^7/_8$ x 4 $^7/_8$. $2.95. For information on our other military pocket guides, see pages 200 and 206 and visit www.veteransworld.com.

Quantity discounts:		
1 copy	$2.95	
10 copies	$23.60	
25 copies	$51.63	
50 copies	$88.50	
100 copies	$147.50	
500 copies	$663.75	
1,000 copies	$1,180.00	
5,000 copies	$5,162.50	
25,000 copies	$22,125.00	
50,000 copies	$36,875.00	
100,000 copies	$59,000.00	

ORDERS AND QUANTITY DISCOUNTS:
1-800-361-1055 or www.impactpublications.com

The Military Guide
to Financial
Independence
& Retirement

Doug Nordman

Impact Publications
Manassas Park, VA

ISBN: 978-1-57023-319-7 (13-digit); 1-57023-319-5 (10-digit)

Library of Congress: 2010941053

Publisher: For information on Impact Publications, including current and forthcoming publications, authors, press kits, online bookstore, and submission requirements, visit the left navigation bar on the front page of the publisher's main company website: www.impactpublications.com.

Publicity/Rights: For information on publicity, author interviews, and subsidiary rights, contact the Media Relations Department: Tel. 703-361-7300, Fax 703-335-9486, or email: query@impactpublications.com.

Sales/Distribution: All bookstore sales are handled through Impact's trade distributor: National Book Network, 15200 NBN Way, Blue Ridge Summit, PA 17214, Tel. 1-800-462-6420. All special sales and distribution inquiries should be directed to the publisher: Sales Department, IMPACT PUBLICATIONS, 9104 Manassas Drive, Suite N, Manassas Park, VA 20111-5211, Tel. 703-361-7300, Fax 703-335-9486, or email: query@impactpublications.com.

Contents

Dedication

TO MY FATHER ... for asking the questions.

TO MY SPOUSE ... for saying "Nords, you have a book in you," and then patiently editing all of it.

TO MY DAUGHTER ... for teaching me more about writing than I ever learned from my high-school composition classes, and for all the waves we've surfed together. You may think you're ready for college, but I wonder if college is ready for you.

Acknowledgments

Books don't write themselves, and writers don't write by themselves.

My deepest thanks to Bob Clyatt and Billy and Akaisha Kaderli, who showed me the way and made the introductions. They offered many thoughtful comments about the book's approach and its audience. And, of course, once I told them what I was going to do, then I actually had to do it.

Big thanks also to SamClem, Bridget Moorman, and Tomcat98. Those seemed like such simple questions! Your thoughts and suggestions helped Bob rip the first draft to shreds, but you made the second draft even better.

Thanks to Ken, Arif, and the rest of the veterans, military families, and early retirees on Early-Retirement.org. You volunteered your stories, offered many topics, and then had to read it all more than once. I may have had a book in me, but you guys pulled it out.

Thanks also to the denizens of "The Bar," who've all been there for each other for over half a decade. (You know who you are.) You've kept me from ripping other things to shreds when I couldn't pull out the words.

Royalty Donations to Military Charities: The author is donating all of this book's royalties to military charities chosen by the book's contributors. See http//The-Military-Guide.com to learn more about the charities being supported with royalties from this book.

"What's money? A man is a success if he
gets up in the morning and goes to bed at night and in
between does what he wants to do."

– Bob Dylan

CONGRATULATIONS! Because of the military's training and benefits, you and your family can become financially independent. You can accumulate enough wealth to only work when you want to. You can live the way you please.

You don't have to win a lottery, inherit a fortune, or execute lucrative stock options. You don't have to be a hyperactive day-trader or even a brilliant investor, and you don't have to live a life of deprivation. A military pension boosts your success but it's not essential. Even if you and your family have only completed one enlistment, your skills and discipline will help you build the foundation of a lifetime of retirement and financial security.

When you're financially independent, you can retire early or work on your own terms until you're ready for a full retirement. The choice is yours.

But the key to retiring early is to start planning early. This book will show you how.

Why This Book?

"Well, Doug, why are you still working?"

That's the question my family and I tried to answer as my military career was ending. I retired in June 2002 at the age of 41, after 20 years of service and as the stock market's bear took a big bite out of our investment portfolio. Everything worked out fine, but the transition had a few speed bumps that we could have avoided with a little more knowledge and better planning.

Life is about not only work, power, and riches beyond our wildest dreams – it's about earning the financial independence to allow people to choose what's right for them. I'm grateful to those who showed me how to become financially independent. I'd like to honor them by helping others, so let's answer the above question as it applies to you.

The first step is to get you to the point where you can ask it! Financial independence gives you the choice to keep working, to pursue your own avocation, or to live the way you please. Once you're eligible for the military pension then you can continue with your service, semi-retire to a second career, or enjoy the early-retirement lifestyle. Even if you're not planning to stick around for the military pension there are still many paths to retirement. This book will show you where to find them.

I read as much as I can about financial independence and retirement. (See the Appendices and the Recommended Reading list.) Eighteen months after I retired, I stumbled across the discussion forum at www.Early-Retirement.org. In 2004 it was only a few hundred strong, and I realized that I was one of only two veterans there who had retired from the military without immediately beginning a second career. I started sharing my thoughts. A few thousand posts later, veterans and other posters said, "You should write a book." Today the forum has only a handful of military early retirees among 8,000 members, but over 70 veterans have contributed their stories to our collective wisdom. Learn from us.

As I learned more about retirement, I realized that I'd already missed a wonderful opportunity to prepare for it almost a decade earlier. Although I stayed on active duty until I was eligible for retirement, I could have resigned from active duty for a Reserve career that would have been every bit as fulfilling, rewarding, and profitable, but with much less stress. I was so busy trying to keep up with work that I never noticed the chance to bring my life and my work into balance. I didn't break free of the "fog of work," but Chapter 7 explains how to watch out for this problem and to be ready for your own opportunities.

A retirement forum is a springboard to an entire library of resources. Once you've read the basics, you can dig into the areas that interest you the most. It's not just about achieving retirement – it's also about choosing the lifestyle to get you there, exploring the options, and learning what brings value to your life. The analysis tools are more flexible and powerful every year. The forum will keep tabs on what's new and you'll be able to get answers to your most obscure questions. Once you achieve your own financial independence and retirement, you can pay it forward to the next group of veterans. You can help write the next edition of early-retirement books!

"Why Plan for the Future? I Could be Killed Tomorrow!"

Of course we hope that never happens. But if good training keeps you alive under the worst possible conditions, then why not apply it to the rest of your life? What about training yourself financially, mentally, and emotionally for retiring when you want to?

This idea is an extension of the lifestyle you've lived since the day you joined the service. As unbelievable as it may seem from within the ranks, the U.S. military is one of the world's best organizations at planning, preparing, and executing. During your service you'll spend thousands of hours reading professional material, preparing for promotion tests, and conducting exercises. You'll maximize your combat effectiveness and then train others how to maximize theirs. You've worked hard for those skills, and you should be proud of them!

So why not use those skills to prepare yourself for the rest of your life? Think of all the possibilities and consider what courses of action you'll need to get there. Don't let a failure to plan end up being a plan to fail. You took charge of your career, so you can learn how to take charge of yourself and your future. This guide will show you how others have done it so that you can too.

A lifetime of occupational drudgery isn't much of an alternative to combat. If you blissfully spend your earnings then you will certainly outlive your savings. However by investing a little **today** and for the rest of your career, you'll give compounding the chance to work its magic. It's slow, it's boring, and for the first couple years it's difficult to see the progress. But saving and investing doesn't have to crimp your lifestyle. By the time you've had enough of working for a paycheck, you may have the financial independence to make your own retirement decision.

Mental preparation for retirement is just as important. Someday you'll be at a tough spot at your duty station, perhaps fighting with the assignment officer over your next billet, dealing with a family crisis, or facing a retirement deadline that you haven't really thought about. Maybe you want to stay on active duty, or maybe, like me, it never even occurred to you to stop working before your 65th birthday. Would you like to be in charge of the all-important retirement decision? If you had the choice and the savings, when would **you** like to retire?

Your emotions can make your retirement transition seem effortless, or they can completely derail the process. How do you feel about retiring? Do you want to start a different career, work part-time, volunteer, or pursue your own interests? Do you discuss it with your family, relatives, and friends? Is it the goal that keeps you going to work each morning, or the fantasy you escape to when you're angry, miserable, and frustrated? You can't emotionally prepare for retirement if you've just been passed over for promotion, if you're fighting the chain of command about your next assignment, or if you're burned out and exhausted. You have to think about it every few months and see if it's the lifestyle you want. You'll need to stop fantasizing and start building a new reality.

As long as you're working, it's worth planning for the worst and hoping for the best. Maybe it's been easier to let the military run your career for you, but someday you're going to have to put yourself in charge of living your life the way that feels right. The earlier you start, the more choices you'll be able to make.

How This Book Can Help

This book was written with the help of dozens of veterans from every service at all stages of their lives. They've mercilessly reviewed my writing and offered many useful suggestions. You don't have to make our mistakes or blaze your own trail – read what we've done and choose what works for **you**.

You'll learn how to set yourself on the path to financial independence and talk about the process of deciding when to retire. We'll review all the vocabulary, explain the military pension rules, and discuss the transition. Although it's easiest when you stick around for the full 20 years, we'll also explain how to retire through the Reserves/National Guard. We'll even tell the stories of families who left the military after just 10 years to semi-retire and live their own lives.

We'll show readers who are considering retirement how to leverage their inflation-adjusted pensions and their military health care to enjoy the way of life that they've spent their careers defending. This guide will smooth the transition to retirement and give you a reference manual for the rest of your life. We'll discuss life/work issues and recommend your options. We'll lay out the transition timeline and explain the choices you and your family face. This book is not "just another benefits guide"! After plotting your own course to retirement, you'll be able to consult dozens of other specialized sources that actual retirees have used for achieving their dreams.

We are offering you a bird's-eye view of the retirement landscape without getting down in the mud and slogging through every little detail. Unlike so many other "military retirement" books, this is not a thinly disguised job-search manual. This is a guide to your goals of financial independence and retirement so that you have the **choice** of pursuing a job search. Instead of re-writing the thousands of pages already offered by other experts, we want to give you the information that you can use **now**. You'll have the basics without digging through stacks of research, and the Recommended Reading list will help you decide what little details you want to slog through on your own.

Although the military pension and benefits greatly smooth the transition to early retirement, they're not always necessary. You'll read real-life stories of veterans who have blazed their own trails without government pensions or military health care.

How to Read This Book

Read the chapters in order or skip around to the parts that interest you. Each career is different and families may have different priorities. We'll start out by discussing how to achieve early retirement after a 20-year active-duty career (that's less complicated!), but feel free to jump ahead to Chapter 5 on Reserve pensions – or no pensions at all.

If you're already a veteran, then treat this book like a technical manual. Enjoy confirming what you already know or skip around to the part you need to solve a problem. Even if you're still on active duty and plan to stay past 20 years of service, you may want to pay particular attention to Chapter 5 on the Reserves/National Guard and the examples of those who have already left the service. It's good to know your options!

If you're just beginning a military career, then you may want to read Chapter 7 first. If you're a family member or if your significant other is a veteran, this is the best way to learn all the material you'll need to get started. It may be hard to visualize yourself in a future that could be 20 years away, but every single retiree wishes that they'd started planning earlier than they actually did.

If you've left active duty for the Reserves or National Guard, then jump to Chapter 5. Don't feel left out if you've decided that the military isn't for you. Skip ahead to Chapter 6 to learn other paths to semi-retirement and early retirement. The military may set you on the road to retirement, but you can get to your destination by many different routes.

If you're within a year of retirement, pay particular attention to the countdown checklists in Chapters 3 and 4. These checklists have a different goal – you're not going to deploy and you might not even be looking for a job! The retirement transition can be both emotionally and mentally challenging for both you and your loved ones. The more time and discussion everyone has, the more realistic their expectations will be. It helps to start planning and saving early, but it helps even more if everyone close to you discusses the subject and supports your efforts.

For those of you with a more analytical (or engineering) perspective, pay attention to the "touchy-feely" sections about preparing yourself emotionally and mentally as well as financially. Speaking as an engineer, I think you'll be glad you did. Believe it or not, your plans may encounter significant skepticism, concern, and even jealousy. You may not be surprised to hear it from your chain of command, but you'll also get it from your friends, your relatives, and even your family. Although financial planning can seem overwhelming at times, the vast majority of discussions on www. Early-Retirement.org talk about how to deal with other people's expectations. You may have to choose between pleasing yourself and pleasing everyone else.

Read this book and learn from it, but execute your plan as soon as possible. Don't wait until you've learned everything and polished it to perfection. Turn your plan into action **now** and adjust it as your career progresses. One of the most important factors in any investment is giving it the time to grow. Compound interest is one of the world's most powerful financial tools, and it can make your retirement – or break it. You may be able to catch up if you're starting late or recovering from a financial disaster, but every day of delay will add weeks or even months to your working years. It can seem like an overwhelming challenge to begin saving for a six-figure portfolio, but the trick is to save early and save regularly. Review the financial suggestions in Chapter 7 and get started. Just as there are many paths to retirement, there are many different types of assets and allocations to get you there!

Once you've gone through all the chapters, work through the Appendices and the Recommended Reading list. Internet addresses and books on the list will be updated on the book's website. http://The-Military-Guide.com. This book was written as a group effort of the veterans of www.Early-Retirement.org, and that discussion board can be your #1 reference. The threads are never boring and the group will answer your questions.

You should also browse this book every few months to see how it affects you and your planning. You may realize that some advice doesn't apply to you, or you may be mentally ready to glean a few more nuggets. If this helps you reach your goal, please tell us and pay it forward to someone else!

When you've achieved financial independence and your retirement goals, please let me know what to tell the next generation. We always appreciate hearing from a new poster on the discussion board, but feel free to e-mail me. NordsNords@gmail.com. I'm only the **first** author of this book, and with your help we'll publish many more editions.

Plan Your Post-Military Life

WHERE ARE YOU GOING? When you're at 15 years of service, what do you see happening in five years? Will you continue on active duty, will you retire from the military and find a "bridge career,"[1] will you semi-retire and work part-time, or will you retire early and never work for a paycheck again?

These fork-in-the-road questions are the tough issues in any retirement decision. Like all tough questions, the answer is "It depends." That may not be the sound bite you want to hear, but it's the only answer that will help you decide what's best for you.

You'll find your own answer for your own reasons (and perhaps for your family), so your decision may not be the "right" one for anyone else. Allow yourself to make a decision and, while you're pursuing it, give yourself the option to change your plan. The job skills that employers truly care about (your leadership, your management experience, and your ethics) won't go stale. I hope that you'll read this book, talk with your family and other people, and think about your goals. Whatever decision you make should be subject to regular review. Don't lock yourself in!

This chapter will help you sort out your priorities and your feelings. Your top priority for retirement is **financial independence**. If you haven't achieved that by the time you've left the service, you'll need to pursue a paid occupation. You won't have the option to stop working. Your next priority is providing for your spouse and kids (if applicable). **Communication** is still the key to keeping everyone happy, just as it is on active duty. After years of sacrifices and deployments, your family may want you around more often, and your idea of supporting them may be quite different from theirs. A career change is a great time to discuss all your options and to renegotiate the family expectations.

Feelings matter almost as much as the priorities, and those emotions will make a big difference in your performance and your health. Feelings are much more difficult to evaluate than the mechanics of making the transition. When you're on active duty, your occupation is probably full of mentors and peers who can tell you precisely where you need to go and exactly how to get there. Some of them are worth listening to, and you probably wish you'd ignored others. However, the best career wisdom I've ever heard was similar to the "It depends" answer: "Do it as long as you're having fun." The idea is that **your performance will be at its peak when you're challenged, fulfilled, and happy**. Peak military performance leads to great evaluations, faster promotions, and even better jobs.

On the other hand we've all met the miserable people who tried to do tours that they weren't suited for (despite their best intentions), or those equally miserable folks who stayed too long. Take it one tour at a time and stop when you can't find anything more that you'd enjoy doing. Leaving the military may be hard, and it's harder to contemplate a few months without a paycheck. However, the hardest task of all is the soul-destroying experience of enduring a tour that has no appeal or fulfillment.

Even outside the military, it's tough to keep your financial and family priorities if you're not having fun. You have to pay attention to your own feelings as you go through your military retirement transition. You'll only succeed at your goals if they make you feel curious, happy, and maybe even excited about chasing them. If you're grimly clenching your jaw and preparing to gut it out for another five years, you may not be making the right choice. You may even be risking your mental, emotional, and physical health.

Watch out for another unhappy situation: **burnout**. It's extremely difficult to make good choices when you're exhausted, frustrated, and miserable. If you feel that retiring is the only way to get out of a terrible job, you may need to reconsider where you're going. Many people pursue a fantasy retirement because they can't imagine putting up with work any longer. When they retire, though, they may find that they haven't developed a lifestyle (or the savings!) to enjoy their new free time. If you have the chance to catch up on sleep, clear your head, and think about all the issues, then you may decide that what you really need is a different assignment or a career change. Don't keep working because you can't imagine what else you could do with yourself, but don't retire just because you're positive that work can't get any worse. You have to move toward a **goal**, not just run away from bad situations.

I've heard from many unhappy people in the military, so let me emphasize the illusion of a fantasy retirement. When you're chronically overworked, overstressed, and suffering low morale, making a retirement decision is an overwhelming impossibility. You can't make good decisions during burn-out. Instead of risking your finances and your lifestyle, find a way to get some time off. It's hard to get two straight weeks of leave to contemplate your future, especially if you're transferring between duty stations, but **you have to find the time**. Don't use that precious leave to clean the house, finish the yard work, or take the big family vacation. You're going to focus your efforts (and your family's discussion) on getting ready for retirement with maybe a bridge career. Catch up on your sleep, spend a couple days winding down, and let the fog clear from your thinking. By the end of the first week, you should be ready to start talking about the issues and considering your decision.

The Biggest Obstacles Confronting All Retirees: Health Care and Inflation

All retirees have to accumulate the resources to last for the rest of their lives, but early retirees (before age 65) have two daunting challenges: paying for health care and contending with decades of inflation as they age.

Health insurance is largely a workplace benefit, and many workers feel "locked into" their jobs by it. Health insurance can be hundreds of dollars per month without an employer's subsidy. The American health care system is the main reason that traditional retirees stay in the workforce until age 65, when Medicare starts to cover many of their health expenses. Even after age 65, retirees still have to contend with rising insurance premiums, higher prescription medication costs, and long-term care concerns.

Inflation is far more insidious. While a health crisis can wipe out a retiree's finances, inflation is at least as deadly because it's hard to notice the corrosive long-term effects. At just 4% a year, a decade of inflation can raise retiree expenses by nearly 50%. Retirees in their 60s may only have to contend with two or three decades of inflation, but retirees in their 40s will have to survive four or five decades of inflation that could easily triple their expenses.

The Biggest Benefits of a Military Retirement: TRICARE and an Inflation-Fighting Pension

The federal government has given military veterans some of the world's best tools for meeting retirement challenges.

It may seem unbelievable but it's a fact: TRICARE, while admittedly beset by flaws and perennial budget challenges, is among the nation's premier affordable health care systems. TRICARE covers far more for active-duty veterans (and their families) than civilian health insurance – while frequently charging far less. Unfortunately, many veterans don't learn this fact until they leave the service, while others with pre-existing conditions may feel locked into military or civil service in order to be able to afford their health care costs. In 2009, an active-duty retiree paid less than $40/month for comprehensive TRICARE family coverage that, for civilian retirees, would cost hundreds or even thousands of dollars.

As good a financial deal as TRICARE may be, the military pension is even better! Military veterans are among the last of the world's occupations to earn a **defined-benefit pension** in an era when employers are moving toward defined-contribution 401(k)s. Despite the risks that we bear to qualify for that government pension, it's paid by one of the world's best-funded institutions with the power to tax its citizens for more revenue and to print its own money.

Not only is the federal government likely to pay military pensions long after corporate pensions hit the skids, but also that pension includes a **cost of living adjustment (COLA)** for inflation. This is extremely rare in the business world. Military pensions (as well as Social Security) rise each year by the inflation rate measured in the Consumer Price Index (CPI). That index may have its own flaws and detractors, but there is no better measure of the nation's inflation. You may experience a personal inflation rate that's smaller (or perhaps bigger) than the CPI, but veterans' pensions will keep up with inflation far better than any other system.

We don't have to depend on the government's marketing. Anyone can buy a CPI-adjusted COLA pension from an insurance company in the form of an annuity. However, these annuities are expensive, difficult to find, filled with restrictions and exceptions, and only backed by the company's ability to pay. You might spend over a million dollars to deliver the value of your military COLA pension.

So where are all the military retirees? And if the military's pension and health care benefits solve the biggest challenges, then why are military early retirees so hard to find?

Where are All the Retirees?
How do We Ask for Their Advice?

Have you ever noticed that the people in your command can help you with just about anything? No matter how obscure your question, there's always someone who knows the answers or can find somebody else who does. While the "soldier network" is great for career or lifestyle advice on active duty, it's not so good for asking questions about retirement. Everyone knows a retired veteran but the details seem a little vague. The retired people must have better things to do with their time because they hardly ever drop by the office. How are they doing? What problems did they have with the transition process? What should we watch out for? Were they ready for retirement? Did they have to get a job, or did they already have enough money to do whatever they wanted to? If they're not working, then what do they **do** all day?

A 2004 study of the U.S. military concluded that only about 15% of the nation's veterans remained on duty for at least 20 years.[2] The number of retired veterans in that 15% who become early retirees (no longer working for pay) is even smaller. After several years of searching, I have only met a handful of people who completely retired after a 20-year career. There are no Department of Defense studies and there is very little other information on the phenomenon. One survey conducted by Russ Graves, a retired officer at Texas A&M University, concluded that 85% of retired officers immediately returned to civilian work after the military.[3] In the more senior ranks, the percentages were even higher!

Semi-retirement and bridge careers are far more common (and more achievable). While a veteran can usually return to full-time employment, if they're financially independent then they can seek employment on their own terms. It may be entrepreneurial, part-time, seasonal, or one contract at a time – but **financial independence** is the key to having the choice.

Whether they're retired early, semi-retired, or working in a bridge career, the retirees are out there. They found a way to do it, and you can too! So let's figure out where they're hiding and get their advice.

One option for finding military retirees is developing your own **network**. As you read shipmates' retirement announcements or sit through their ceremonies, ask if you can contact them in a few months. You want to learn what retirement surprises they encountered and they'll be happy to share their new lifestyle. They may have embarked on a bridge career, but you'll gain their perspective on how their military pension and health care benefits have eased their transition.

The **Retired Activities Office** (or Retirement Service Office) at your local base is another option. Their mission is to help retirees solve problems. They also coordinate volunteer efforts, so the staff has a long list of retiree contacts and they'll be happy to pass along your questions.

By far the best place to find military retirees is on **Internet discussion boards**. A huge veteran's network has grown over the last decade to share information on benefits, reunions, and memories. While enjoying tracking down old wingmen, find out if they've retired early or if they're in a bridge career. Veterans will also post on Internet early-retirement discussion boards. See the Recommended Reading section for the largest boards and their website addresses.

What They Don't Tell You at the Military's Transition Assistance Programs

When I was thinking about retirement, I was frustrated by the military's transition assistance programs.

First, I had to attend the class before my retirement request could be approved. Second, it was inconvenient. During a very busy workweek, at the cusp of a crucial life decision, I was expected to sit in a crowded classroom for presentations on veteran's benefits. Finally, I wasn't comfortable thinking about the next step. I wanted leisure time to rest, recuperate, and think. I didn't want to cram everything into a three-day seminar.

Then I realized that we'd been learning a little about our health care benefits and our pension, but most of the talks were about starting a bridge career! The "retirement transition" was from a military career to a civilian career. We'd heard all the right phrases: "Build your network." "Target your company." "Dress for success." "May I present my card?" It dawned on me that I'd already had a career for the last couple of decades, thank you, and I didn't really want another one. Why was I still working?

The transition counselors can't help with this question. Most of the veterans attending the class are leaving the service before they're eligible for a military retirement. Even among the military retirees, most haven't become financially independent and aren't ready to handle the concept of a bridge career. Complete early retirement seems like a fantasy, not a plan, and almost no one wants to discuss it during the transition process.

Nearly a decade later, though, I appreciate the military's transition programs for what they can't do as well as for what they can do. Human beings tend to resist change, and leaving the military is perhaps the biggest life change since we entered the military. The transition process forces us to focus our attention on something that we might wish to avoid. Our government and the taxpayers don't want to see homeless veterans sleeping under highway overpasses, either, so vocational assistance can make everyone feel that we're equipped to handle our new lives.

Finally, the **most important benefit** of the transition programs is to prod you to take charge of your life. You can contemplate your new life – and determine whether your finances will support it. You can be responsible for your own entertainment. You can start a bridge career if you want to, or you can take some time off. Sitting in that transition classroom will make you realize that you have to do it for yourself instead of letting your chain of command take care of you for the rest of your life.

DON'T EXPECT the military's transition programs to answer all your questions. You may be subject to seemingly pointless activities or even criticism. One retiring officer was required to participate in "dress for success" day and was not amused to be tactfully informed that her business attire exposed excess cleavage. You may even be chastised for not taking the career search seriously enough. You should bring your own list of benefits questions to work on, your own medical issues to research, and maybe even your own resume to update. Don't expect the seminar agenda to walk you through the steps that are important to you. You might even need to keep your head down, stay quiet, and avoid eye contact.

Which do You Want? An Occupation, a Bridge Career, or an Avocation?

The biggest difference among those terms is that occupations are the series of activities that form careers and avocations. We've all had jobs that have given us a life lesson, even if our only learning was a strong desire not to repeat that job. Many of us started our first jobs to pay the bills or to get the experience to step up to better jobs. For some workers, jobs aren't a reason to live – only a means to some other end.

Careers are occupations with training and experience. Remember the Navy's old recruiting slogan, "It's not a job, it's an adventure!"? Anyone can find a job to pay the bills, but those who join the service want something more. A career offers greater challenges and more rewards than a job. A bridge career, which we'll discuss in more detail shortly, bridges the gap between your military career and full retirement.

Avocations are the best of all: your life's pursuit of happiness. They're all the military slogans that we know so well. They're the fascinating missions you can't believe you're paid for and the challenges that you'd tackle for fun. When you've reached 20 years of service, you know that you've had a career. However, when you wish that you were able to keep going beyond 40 years, it's an avocation. Many lawyers, doctors, and investors practice their craft until they're no longer physically or mentally capable.

Early retirees claim that early retirement is their avocation.

Veterans may have an additional avocation: a commitment to service. After decades of completing missions and saving lives, it's very difficult to walk away from a lifestyle that protects our society. It's also very difficult to stop taking care of others. People's needs may be very important to the happiness of veterans who have been taking care of their troops and keeping others safe.

If service is so important to you that you're willing to subject yourself to employment, then you could continue your avocation with a paycheck. You should also consider the alternatives of volunteer service or nonprofit work. Whether you serve your commitment through a bridge career or though volunteering during retirement, you can enjoy the knowledge that you've found your true avocation under all the workplace distractions.

Bridge Careers

The idea of a "bridge career" comes from Marc Freedman, the author of *Prime Time* and *Encore*. A firm believer in working, Freedman can't even conceive of retiring if one enjoys the challenges and the success of working. With many civilians leaving their careers in their 50s or even their 40s, he advocates a second career to bridge the years and take willing workers into their 70s.

For most retired military, finances are the reason for a bridge career: you need the money to build up your investment portfolio and to reach financial independence (FI). Even when you're FI, though, there's a world of fulfilling (paid) employment and volunteer work to explore. One well-known example is the military's "Troops to Teachers" program (http://www.proudtoserveagain.com), and industry is following the lead of the educators. AARP works with large corporations like Wal-Mart and Home Depot to offer flexible hours, seasonal work, and even different locations as you travel around the country.

Another bridge career option is semi-retirement. Bob Clyatt, the groundbreaking author of *Work Less, Live More*, uses occasional employment for both his lifestyle and his finances. You may turn your passion into a paying hobby (as he has) or work seasonally in a specialty or new skill. It may be as straightforward as working holiday retail or preparing tax returns. It could be as complicated as offering contract support for military exercises or developing your own business. No matter how hard you choose to work at it, semi-retirement affords you the option of working to carry your portfolio through rough markets or to save up for special expenses.

"BOXKICKER" WRITES online about retiring from active duty as an E-7: "After 20+ years of the hustle and bustle of military life, I have really enjoyed the almost stress-free lifestyle of having my hair long, waking up when I want, and playing golf when I want. I am 40 years old and I don't want to burn my bridges too soon. I really could do this forever and not be bored at all, but will my finances be enough forever?

continued

I'm three credit hours short of a bachelor's degree and I have 35 months of GI Bill remaining for more degrees or training. I want to get a master's degree in sports management just to learn about something I enjoy...SPORTS! I would love to work for a pro, college, or high school team. Even working in a community center running their recreation programs would be fun! My ultimate job would be to work as a golf course manager.

My pension is $1,880/month with a COLA. I'm currently working 20-30 hours a week at the local military base golf course for $7.50/hour. I umpire/referee local high school sports for $25-$55/game. I made $2,200 in six weeks during baseball season and $600 in four weeks of basketball. I rent a home with my fiancée and her three teenagers, who she's raising on her income (and child support). I have two car payments and no other debt. I only have $45K in my TSP account and less than $10K in my IRA.

I really enjoy being semi-retired, but sometimes I wonder if this will run out. Should I get another job to stay marketable in case I need to go to work?

I wish I could just keep working at the golf course and going to school. It is fun, and doesn't even feel like work. I am really content where I am. Working in the corporate world doesn't interest me at all. I am not a cubicle kind of guy, nor do I want to travel to far-off lands. I had enough of that on active duty.

I live a pretty frugal lifestyle and I enjoy it. I am a homebody. If I can play golf, I am happy! It would always be nice to have some savings built up, but I really don't want to bend over backwards and WORK to get it. I enjoy being retired military and having a steady pension with inexpensive health care insurance."

Career Surveys and Assessment Tests

The military's transition process has many tools beyond the classroom briefs. Surveys and assessments are excellent ways to figure out if another career is in the cards. Not only do the tools help explain military skills in civilian terms, but they also let veterans brainstorm other occupations, bridge careers, and avocations. This is the chance to discover what you want to do when you grow up. If you're excited by the possibilities then you're probably not yet ready for early retirement. However if you're bored and frustrated by the discovery process then you have a very significant indicator that you may be ready to consider early retirement. One of the best ways to learn about early retirement is to take a three-month vacation, but it's difficult to get a leave of absence from the military. Without a few months' time off, the transition tools may be your best indicator of whether you're ready to take matters into your own hands.

ONE MILITARY base filled a conference room with transition planners and computer guides. A nuclear engineering officer, a self-taught expert on finding another job, had finished researching all the options and understood the strengths and weaknesses of each tool. After many nights and weekends of flipping paperwork or clicking through the software, the "career interest surveys" and the "self-assessment guides" claimed that he'd make an excellent mid-level manager or a nuclear engineer – golly, maybe both! This was not the hoped-for fresh start. There probably wouldn't be deployments or midwatches, but the uniform would be office attire and there would still be the occasional weekend duty. He'd had enough of that and was ready for a change.

Objections to Early Retirement

The military's retirement system has a number of advantages for retirees, but if so few veterans seek early retirement then you may rightfully hesitate. What are you missing?

One element is the approval of society. Test this yourself by telling a few shipmates, neighbors, or relatives that you're considering early retirement. You won't get congratulatory handshakes or backslaps. Instead, you're fantasizing! They haven't even attempted your planning or your hard work for this goal. They may have also decided that early retirement is out of their reach, and they may not be happy to hear that you're doing it when they're not. It's far more likely that their "helpful comments" could derail your early-retirement goal.

Before you tackle the objections, consider how you'll picture yourself for the next few decades. This is your chance to enjoy your freedom and to develop your maximum personal potential. You should feel as excited about the next phase of your life as you were when you joined the military! What's your personal philosophy about continuing to work? How will you describe yourself? Are you an entrepreneur? A private investor? A surf bum? All of the above? Are you taking a few years off to explore your options, or are you going back to school? Are you going to travel the world or be an at-home parent? You may be able to say, "I'm a retired aviator," but who are you and what are you doing **now**? More importantly, are you planning to be this way until you die, or will you take it one decade at a time?

Once you think about the big picture, you're ready to tackle these "objections":

> *"You're too young to be put out to pasture.*
> *You have so much ahead of you!"*

Yes, you're young if you're retiring before age 65, and one aphorism claims that youth is wasted on the young. Do you really want to "save" retirement for old age, or would you rather learn more about it while you're young? A few months of early retirement will help you recover from a career of chronic fatigue and decide what you want to do with the rest of your life. Corporate dominance and riches beyond your wildest dreams may not be your goal, but perhaps you'll discover another way to serve humanity. You'll still have things that you'll want to see and do before you're too old to be capable of achieving them. Travel and triathlons do not improve with age.

> *"Can't you find a **real** job?"*

Absolutely, and your military record stands on its own merits. You have the skills that employers will compete for, but a better question is whether you **want** a "real" job. Do you still care about trying to work your way to the top of yet another chain of command? The military is certainly different from most people's concept of a real job, and you can seek more alternatives. If you're financially independent, you can pursue your goals without having to take jobs that don't interest you. You can also eliminate many of the irritants that accompany conventional occupations – commuting, office attire, department meetings, working lunches, late hours, and working weekends.

The best benefit of early retirement is gaining the time to pursue an activity other than a "real job." You can volunteer, go to school, learn a new avocation, spend more time with family, travel, entertain yourself, or choose among hundreds of other activities. This is a rare opportunity to figure out what you'd like to do with the rest of your life. It doesn't have to involve a paycheck.

"Who wants to spend all day golfing?"

This question claims that you'll run out of things to do and get bored. If golf is a fascinating activity that keeps you busy most of the week, then enjoy yourself! You can also pick up spare change from tournaments (and your over-optimistic golfing buddies). But like any hobby you should only golf if you enjoy it, and you shouldn't get tired of it. The solution is to brainstorm your interests and to figure out what you want to do with your time. The Recommended Reading section lists several guides to help you rediscover having fun.

"You'll lose all your friends!"

That may be the case. Military retirement will certainly help you tell the difference between your real friends and your co-workers. If people are put off by your early retirement instead of being happy for you, then perhaps they're not such good friends after all.

Most retirees keep in touch with only one or two of their former co-workers. You'll find new interests to share beyond office talk. You'll have plenty of new free time to spend with family, relatives, neighbors, and old shipmates. Your schedule may be wide open, too, and you'll be the person they can count on to be available next Tuesday afternoon.

You probably moved around a lot in your military career and you eventually made new friends. Now in early retirement, as you spend more time on activities that you enjoy, you'll still find new friends.

"You're going to retire NOW, in the middle of all this?!? But you're up for promotion next year and the team needs you!!"

(Thanks to SamClem on www.Early-Retirement.org for this one!)

You may feel that you're letting down your boss (who recommended you for schools or special recognition) or your wingmen (who would be even more overworked without you), or you may feel like a quitter. You may have been recently promoted with even greater career potential. Maybe you really should stick around for a few more years?

These self-doubt questions are natural, and the chain of command may even try to use them to change your mind. No one enjoys personnel changes, and it's easier for them to hold on to you than to train your replacement – if they can even find your replacement.

Don't get distracted by these red herrings. The **real** question is what's best for you and your family. Every promotion already recognizes your **potential** to do the more demanding work, but it's your decision to continue to live up to that standard. Your chain of command would eventually be reluctant to have your service if your heart was no longer in it. Your family has sacrificed a lot to support you to this point and they may feel that they've supported you and the military for long enough. How much longer will they put up with your duty?

Your co-workers, if they're truly your friends, would much rather see you escape from the asylum than continue to suffer with your fellow inmates. (You'll always be able to get together to commiserate over a frosty beverage or two.) As for the rest of your peers, they're tired of competing with you for the next promotion – they'll be happy that you've made room for them to advance!

"You'll lose all your contacts, and you won't be able to get a job!"

The implicit concern of this statement is that a valuable asset is wasted. Those contacts helped start a career and helped you figure out how to get things done. A database shouldn't be discarded!

If you feel that you can't give up your contacts then you may be more interested in a bridge career. Those contacts provided crucial steps to your military retirement, but eventually you'll have to become a mentor emeritus or even disengage from the network. If they're really your friends, however, then you'll still socialize even when you're not talking about work. Besides, now they can use your advice on the retirement process.

Although you're leaving "your" network, you're also developing a new network of different contacts. You may be volunteering, traveling, or finding new local activities. You'll meet new people and you'll have the time to get to know them. Best of all, your true friends from your working days will still be with you.

STORY 1: One financially independent veteran says, "The hard part I'm finding is the pressure/temptation to take a government or contractor job while the 'iron is hot' – while my connections and experience are current." This struggle is especially difficult if a military retirement is forced by high-year tenure, a family situation, or some other ultimatum. If this issue is one of your top retirement concerns, it may be best to continue work, even part-time, until you feel more comfortable about your decision.

STORY 2: SamClem retired from the military after 21 years. He kept working for his family's goals of paying their kid's college tuition and building a safety net of additional savings for more travel and luxuries. His potential was directly related to the skills and contacts he made during his final tour of duty, and his job opportunity would disappear after a few months. He was offered plenty of jobs, but if he waited too long, the only remaining work would be for lower pay. Although their calculations show that they're financially independent, he plans to work for only a few more years to gain the peace of mind to last a lifetime.

STORY 3: Deserat, a Reservist, was activated by her service. She took a leave of absence from her civilian career, moved to another country, and did a totally different job for nearly four years. When she returned to her civilian job, turnover was low and over 80% of her co-workers were still there. Her network was intact, but she returned with a better perspective, more skills, and a new set of active-duty contacts to add to her old network. She was much more effective at her civilian career, with the credibility and the pay to reflect that.

"You'll be so bored."

It's quite possible. Retirement means that you're responsible for your own entertainment. (Don't expect your spouse to volunteer for this duty!) However, it also means that you get to change the channel and try something different.

As a kid you had interests, hobbies, and activities that kept you busy from sunup to sundown. Some days were probably so busy that you couldn't find the time for unpleasant things like household chores or part-time jobs. You had no trouble pursuing your own path. Now it's time to return to that halcyon era!

Many retirees still make lists of goals and things "To Do." You can be extremely specific ("run a half-marathon by June 30th") or more general ("short-term goal: run a 10K"), and you're the only scorekeeper. Most retirees also discover that their goals are too aggressive and their deadlines are too soon, so they relax a bit and move in smaller increments over longer times.

During the first few months of retirement you'll have plenty of problems to solve and activities to complete. Eventually, though, the major decisions are made, the lists settle down, and you'll be crossing off those goals. If you've discovered a bunch of new interests and hobbies, then you'll continue this cycle indefinitely. If nothing new has captured your interest, look at the books and websites on the Recommended Reading list. One or more of them will start your brainstorming and you'll soon fill up your own list.

"Your spouse [significant other, kids,
relatives] will never allow it!"

I hope that you've discussed retirement with your family and reached a consensus before telling anyone else. Communicating will make or break your plan, and early retirement is an emotionally loaded subject that takes time to accept. Share your FI (Financial Independence) numbers so that everyone understands the situation (and maybe catches your mistakes). Reassure younger children that you have enough savings and that everyone will help keep an eye on the budget. You also have to reassure your loved ones that you'll be capable of figuring out your own entertainment. Your spouse may have married you for better or worse, but not necessarily for lunch!

2

You've Decided to Retire!
So, Calculate Your Income

CONGRATULATIONS ON your decision to retire! As the recruiter said all those years ago, the rest is just details.

Ok, I'm Going to Retire From Active Duty.
What do I do Now?

Let's start with the "simplest" case – retiring from active duty. Active-duty retirees are immediately eligible for TRICARE health insurance and a pension, although even this seemingly straightforward decision has some timing considerations. Chapters 5 and 6 describe Reserve retirements (with some benefits when retirement is filed plus a pension at age 60) and completely separating from the services before retirement (NO benefits or pension). First, we'll go through the decisions that can dramatically affect the timing of your retirement as well as its quality. Chapters 3 and 4 describe a basic countdown timeline and various options.

Humor: Things You Shouldn't Learn
to do Before You Retire

Maybe you're retiring because the fun has stopped and you're ready for a change. The family conflicts are piling up and you want to spend more time with your kids. You're thinking about new activities and deciding what you're going to do with your new life. You're reading the books, you're making a list, and you're looking forward to the last day of work! Financial independence has a way of broadening your horizons while reducing your tolerance for workplace follies.

But maybe you're one of those people who have already found new activities, and now work is standing in the way of your new life. You're looking forward to the last day of work because you want to devote all of that "work time" to your new priorities.

The most common example is outdoor activities. It's hard to report to an institutional office building (especially command bunkers without windows) when the sun is shining and the sky is incredibly blue. The mountains need hiking, the golf course needs playing, and the surf is just going to waste. In these circumstances it's certainly understandable if you show up a bit late, need to leave a bit early, or just take a day off! Isn't it?

Not so fast. Remember that your commitment and your work ethic got you to the finish line of this marathon. This is not the time to start cutting corners and turning into one of those deadwood "retired on active duty" veterans. There will be plenty of sunshine in your retirement, and you'll also have years to reflect on how you handled your final months of active duty. When you look back, you want to be confident that you put out your best effort to complete your assigned duties and made sure that someone was ready to take over for you. Take a little leave if it's appropriate, but keep plugging away until that day when the troops have to handle things on their own. In a few more months you'll be taking more leave than you ever imagined possible.

Burnout and laziness are bad enough. While you may be eager to start your new life, **don't get ahead of yourself**. You want to be ready to give all those new activities your full attention and your best effort. Work is probably not compatible with that goal, and you may not be able to handle both activities at the same time. (This is especially true if you're planning a major physical activity.) As you approach retirement, closing out your working life takes top priority. Many of the things you need to do during your final months will be difficult (or even impossible) to complete after retirement. If you just can't wait to begin your new life, consider taking small steps that don't interfere with work. Change your exercise program to build up your endurance for your new activities. Spend more time with your family talking about your new lives and planning your activities. Make lists, schedules, and appointments. But keep your eye on your IN box, complete your checklist **before** you retire, and make sure that none of those projects will be chasing you into retirement.

I SPENT MOST of a Navy career blissfully ignorant of surfing. At the final duty station in Hawaii, however, it was hard to miss. Co-workers would grumble longingly about the surf they saw on the way to work, and some would call in sick with a four-to-six-foot fever. There was already plenty on my "Retirement To-Do" list, but I added surfing lessons.

The first session was on the first day of retirement. Our whole family rented longboards and paddled out together for a lifeguard's helping push into the waves. During the next hour everyone managed to get at least one standup ride before our newly discovered shoulder muscles cramped with exhaustion. I belatedly realized that the retirement budget needed to include a lifetime supply of surfboards and wax.

Today, every morning starts with the surf forecast. Surfing went from a mysterious culture to become a way of life that never would have peacefully co-existed with work. Although I regret missing all those years of surfing while I was on active duty, I'm glad that I didn't have to maintain a work-surf balance!

The Department of Defense Military Retirement Pay System

Before you build your retirement checklist, you need to decide when you're going to retire, and then determine how much you're going to get. The military's retirement pay system seems to be one of the most confusing financial arrangements on the face of the earth, but it has to cover the individual situations of millions of servicemembers. Luckily it's also simpler than it appears to be. Although this section covers the highlights and most of the details, only you can become the leading expert on your own paycheck and benefits. The remainder of this chapter is a road map to figuring out your own pay structure. It shows you how to check that the system is paying you correctly.

In addition to what you learn here, remember to confirm everything you're told about your pay. Follow this chapter's links to the websites and make sure you understand how your retirement pay will be calculated. Ask your pay clerks to show you where the rules are written in the references and make sure those particular rules actually apply to your situation. Your local pay office and the Defense Finance and Accounting Service (DFAS) website (www.dfas.mil) can provide a detailed estimate of your retirement pay based on your service record. It will not only confirm what you've learned here but also it will help you verify your pay record. If the estimates tell you a different number than you're calculating on your own, there could be an error in your pay record. The time to correct those errors is **before** you retire, as frustrating as that may be, since errors take much more time and effort to correct after you retire.

IN THE LATE 1990s all the services moved to a joint pay management system. The consolidation took months to verify that each new pay calculation correctly applied all the services' rules from their old individual systems, and some details inevitably slipped through the cracks. One of the changes assumed that all officers entered the service on the day they were commissioned instead of on the day that they actually started training. At the military academies the graduating classes of 1981-1984 (from nearly two decades ago) were assigned incorrect dates. Retirees of those classes had to correct their service entry date, a detail that took up to three months of processing for thousands of officers. The payoff, however, was an additional 5% of their retirement checks for the rest of their lives.

Don't reach for your calculator yet. First, we'll discuss the three existing retirement systems and how they apply to you. Next, we'll walk through the steps of calculating your retired pay, and finally we'll show some examples. You don't have to do this on your own, either; the Department of Defense (DoD) will do it for you as part of the retirement process and through their website calculators (http://militarypay.defense.gov/retire ment/calc/).

If you've been in the military for a few years, you're probably an expert on the pay system. However, if you're a spouse trying to understand what goes into a retirement pension, then the following details may seem trivial and overly complicated. Keep reading; once you've been through the descriptions and examples, you can check your own pension math by using the websites and online calculators listed in this chapter.

Let's begin with the data that goes into the calculation. Your retirement pay is calculated from two things:

- The date you entered the service

- Your "service multiple" (we'll have more on that in a few pages)

The date you entered the service determines which system you retire under: Final Pay, High Three, or Career Status Bonus (REDUX).

1. Final Pay: If you entered the service before 8 September 1980, your retirement pay is based on the latest pay scale for your rank and your years of service. This system only applies to a small percentage of today's armed forces. (Even if it doesn't apply to you, it also lets us work through a simpler example of calculating retired pay.) Under this pay scale a slight delay in your retirement date, whether for service longevity or the next pay raise or your total time in your highest rank, will make a difference that compounds for the rest of your life. If you have some control over the date of your retirement, it's strongly recommended that you calculate the effect of different dates and compare them to your budget. A small change in the pay scale could make a big difference over the next 50 years. On the other hand, your retirement date may also determine whether you impact your spouse's job, your kid's high school graduation, or how long you have to hang on with that demanding boss – so it's ultimately a personal decision with a financial aspect. The example on pages 38 and 39 shows the impact of taking retirement a few months earlier than financially appropriate.

2. High Three: If you entered the service between 8 September 1980 and 31 July 1986, your pension is based on the weighted average of the pay scales in effect for your final 36 months of active duty. In addition, your first cost-of-living adjustment (COLA) after retirement is reduced by 1% from the Consumer Price Index (CPI) estimate of inflation. Annual pay raises and service longevity aren't as significant under the High Three system, but your time in rank could still make a big difference. You'll want to check the dates of the next raises and your time in rank, calculate the resulting retirement amounts, and compare them to your budget. Keep in mind that your final 36 months of pay may be spread across three different annual pay scales and at least one biennial longevity pay raise. The data will be in DFAS's archives and on your old pay statements, but remember to check each against the other to verify that your pay record is accurate.

3. Career Status Bonus: This system applies to everyone who entered the military on or after 1 August 1986. Originally called REDUX, it promises a $30,000 bonus in the 15th year of service in exchange for a long-term reduction in benefits. REDUX base pay is still calculated on the High Three system, but up to age 62 the pension is usually smaller and COLAs are reduced by one percentage point from the CPI. DoD initially implemented the system for all veterans who joined the service after the August 1986 start date. By the year 2000 Congress was alarmed at the military's sinking retention and changed REDUX to the Career Status Bonus system. This pension system is the same as High Three but with the option of converting to REDUX. Later in this chapter we'll explain why REDUX is a money-losing idea.

HANGING ON for a few more months affects your pension for the rest of your life.

Dan felt that he was ready to retire but he was flexible about the date. He was eligible to retire, he was past his last longevity pay raise, and he had enough time in service to retire at his current rank. Although he was attracted by the idea of retiring in December and starting a brand new year as a brand new retiree, he decided to stay on another month for next year's increase to the military pay tables. It would only be 2.2%, but he expected to be receiving that extra amount in his retirement paycheck for a long time.

When the new pay tables were published, he realized that he could be getting a lot more than he expected. His service had decided to try to persuade people of his rank to stay on active duty by "targeting" them with an extra pay raise that April. Dan wasn't persuaded to stick around past April, but his longevity made him eligible for the same 8.3% raise that all the others at his rank were getting. Delaying his retirement by an extra four months raised his retirement pay by 10.5% for the rest of his life!

Since the retirement systems are based on your service date, make sure that your Date of Initial Entrance to Military Service (DIEMS) is correct. This is usually the date that you were handed your very first ID card. It may be earlier than your Pay Entry Base Date (PEBD) if:

- you had broken service

- you started your service in the Reserves and mobilized to active duty

- you were commissioned through ROTC/service academies

These different dates have already caused many mistakes to be made at recruiting offices and training commands. As the military services converted to the defense joint pay system, not all of these dates correctly transferred to the new formats. There's only a 5% difference between the Final Pay and High Three systems, but it adds up fast when it compounds over decades of retirement.

Once you've determined your retirement system, you'll enter the pay tables to select the highest pay that you expect to receive for your rank and years of service (Final Pay), or you'll calculate the average of your final 36 months of pay (High Three). Remember that the High Three average will include at least one and possibly two longevity raises as well as the calendar-year raises.

Now that you've located your final pay scale or calculated your High Three average, you're ready to apply your service multiple. If you're retiring with 30 years of service, your service multiple is 75%. If you're between 20 and 30 years, then it's 2.5% times your years of service, with each leftover month counting as 1/12 of a year. (If you had 23 years and 5 months of active duty, your multiple would be 2.5% x (23 + 5/12) = 58.54%.) If you took the REDUX retirement option (this is usually a bad idea), your service multiple is reduced by 1/12 of a percent for each month of service less than 30 years. The reduction means that if you're retiring at 20 years of service under REDUX, your service multiple is only 40% instead of 50%.

Finally, your retired pay is calculated by multiplying your Final Pay or High Three pay by the appropriate service multiple. See the sample calculation on page 38.

2007 WAS another landmark year for military retirements and perhaps the most significant change since REDUX was introduced in 1986. The pay charts were extended to 40 years of service (instead of 30), which means that extremely senior veterans can still

continued

look forward to more longevity raises. The service multiple has been raised beyond 75% for more than 30 years of service. If you think that you'll make the rank, then you'll have to decide whether your extra service time is worth a higher military pension. You'll hopefully also be able to save and invest more from your years of extra salary, which has a powerful compounding effect in both your Thrift Savings Plan account and your taxable accounts.

The resulting pension amount can be a bitter disappointment after years of hearing that "You can retire on half of your paycheck." Most active-duty military retiree paychecks will be just 25-40% of the paycheck they're receiving now. That's because the only pay input to the calculation is base pay – not food allowances, housing allowances, uniform allowances, special pay, bonus pay, or anything else. As you approach retirement, you can earn a six-figure annual salary one year and only receive $25,000 the next. It seems like a pretty high price to pay for your freedom!

However, and this is a **big** difference, the seemingly puny retirement check includes a benefit that counters one of a retiree's biggest challenges: **inflation.** You receive a cost-of-living adjustment (COLA) from your first full year of retirement until you die, and that COLA is linked to the same CPI used by the Social Security system. Depending on the inflation rate, you may even get a bigger retirement pension raise than your shipmates get from their annual active-duty pay raise!

We veterans have trouble appreciating the benefits of a COLA pension because we don't experience the alternatives. The vast majority of American pensions (if a retiree is even receiving a pension!) do not have inflation protection. In as little as one decade after retirement, at a seemingly modest annual inflation rate of 3%, a fixed pension will erode to only 74% of the purchasing power of its starting value. If inflation is 5% (the average annual rate from 1970 to 2000), then 10 years later that non-COLA pension will be reduced to only 60% of its value. (See Appendix A on page 148.) Civilians who have been retired for 30 or more years on a fixed pension find that it barely pays for their entertainment budget, let alone their groceries. Military retirees receive annual boosts intended to preserve their purchasing power in perpetuity. The CPI calculation is an imperfect estimate and the subject of considerable controversy, but it's the best system in existence. (Ask any civilian retiree if they wish they had a COLA pension.) If you're still unsure of the benefit of a COLA pension, ask a financial advisor, investment broker, or an insurance company to price the premium cost of an annuity with and without a COLA feature. (See Appendix E on page 163.) There's a big difference in fees.

Here's another caveat: you can still wipe out your COLA by taking the REDUX bonus. Yet it seems like such a winner at your 15th year of service! If you agree to a smaller service multiple and give back 1% of your COLA each year between retirement and age 62, then the Department of Defense will hand you a check for $30,000. At age 62 you'll receive a "catch-up" adjustment to your COLA, so REDUX reductions seem like a pittance alongside that big $30,000 chunk of cash. The catch is that compounding makes all the difference, and DoD hopes that you haven't bothered to check the math. If you retire at age 37 on 40% of your base pay and give back 1% of your COLA for the next 25 years, then by age 62 your pension will only have 62% (four-fifths of 78%) of the purchasing power of its High Three equivalent. You may be able to overcome that drag (after taxes) if you dump your REDUX bonus into a stock index fund for 35 years (see the discussion on page 39 and in Appendix D on page 160). Unfortunately the vast majority of REDUX recipients choose to invest their $30,000 in paying off debt, a home down payment, or…a pickup truck. The REDUX bonus may be a lifesaver if you're struggling with credit-card debt, buying a home, or starting a business, but don't waste it on consumer goods. Don't take DoD's word for it – build a spreadsheet, crunch the numbers, and figure out which scenario will work in your favor. (See Appendix D again and read the REDUX articles in the Recommended Reading section.) Then ask yourself if you trust the DoD to do the right thing years later at your 62nd birthday.

Is the military pension's COLA, in effect since 1963, really worth the effort? Military.com summarized the COLA's effects in a March 2008 article by columnist Tom Philpott.[1] They found that retirees of 1998 drew lower pay than those who retired in 2008 by roughly $200-$300/month for the same rank and years of service. However the retirees of '98 were still ahead of those who retired in 2001 (the first year of High Three retirees) by roughly $100/month. Those who retired in 1973 fared best of all, though, due to years of high-inflation COLAs in the 1980s while military pay raises weren't keeping up. Despite the 1990s decade of active-duty pay increases, the 1973 retirees still earned a bit more than those who retired in 2008. Not only did their COLA shield them from 35 years of inflation but also three decades of compounding even put them slightly ahead of the military's current pay system.

What the Transition Assistance Program (TAP) Can Do for You – and What It Can't

TAP is a wonderful wake-up call. It's required for all separating/retiring veterans, so you can't go home without it. Your chain of command has to leave you alone for a few days and you have to leave your IN box back at your office. (Put away that BlackBerry, too!) Your spouse can attend with you, so two pairs of eyes and ears can help make sure you don't miss anything. Your fellow TAP attendees will also share their stories and the counselors will be able to help you research the answers to your specific questions, so it's a much better resource than randomly browsing military websites.

Repeating what I said in the introduction, human beings tend to resist change – and leaving the military is perhaps the biggest life change since you entered the military. The most important benefit of the transition programs is to prod you to take charge. You can determine whether your finances will support your new life. You can be responsible for your own entertainment. You can start a bridge career if you want to, or you can take some time off. Sitting in that transition classroom will make you realize that you have to make the transition for yourself instead of letting your chain of command take care of you for the rest of your life.

Unfortunately the transition programs can't do the work for you. You may be handed a notebook with a generic checklist, but you'll have to add the details that apply to your specific situation. You may learn about medical and vocational assistance, but you have to research your records and make the appointments. And while they may be able to help you figure out what your pension will be, you have to determine if that's enough to make you financially independent.

See Chapter 4 (page 52) for a discussion of more actions to take during TAP.

Advance Planning

Listen to the trailblazers: by far the most common comment of the new posters on www.Early-Retirement.org and other Internet retirement discussion boards is "I wish I'd started saving and planning sooner!" That's not much consolation if you're reading this during your 19th year of military service, but the good news is that you still have time to let the magic of compound interest work in your favor. You can also make other lifestyle decisions that will accelerate your retirement date.

The next few sections will talk about financial-planning issues that are specific to the military and to early retirees. The discussion will assume that you have some experience with the basics of saving, investing, asset allocation, and budgeting. If this is your first hard look at these concepts, then you have some Recommended Reading to do from the back of this book. If you're familiar with the basics, you're going to learn about ways to optimize your investing and spending to take advantage of your new military and retirement assets.

Financial Myths of Retirement

MYTH #1: Amount of Retirement Income

"You'll need 80% of your pre-retirement income for retirement spending."

This canard comes from 1980s research that found the cost of commuting, childcare, and office attire was about 20% of employment-related expenses. The financial press picked up a great sound bite and turned it into a rule of thumb.

Once again, "it depends." The reality is that you may need as little as 25% or as much as 150% of your pre-retirement income, and you can control a great deal of that variance. This is especially complicated if you're earning special pays, bonuses, or other allowances. Your retirement expenses will depend on the size of your family, your housing costs, your entertainment and travel spending, and your retirement area's cost of living. Don't even waste your time looking at the percentages. Your time will be much better spent figuring out where you're going to retire, what activities you want to spend money on, and what your budget might look like. Then you can figure out how much you'll have to save!

MYTH #2: Avoiding Risks

"Avoid risk by diversifying. You have to invest xx% of your retirement portfolio in stocks, another xx% in bonds, another xx% in commodities, and..."

"Risk tolerance drops with age. Your stock asset allocation should be '120 minus your age' and should be adjusted every year."

"Individual stocks are for losers. They're too risky."

"You can handle the risk of individual stocks and bonds. You have to steer your asset allocation around the yield curve, unless interest rates go down, but then..."

Whether or not you understand this vocabulary, once again, "it depends." Asset allocation is one of the most important factors in the return of an investment portfolio (see Appendix F on page 167), but that allocation depends on how hard you want to work at it and your tolerance for various types of risks.

Some investors are absolutely fascinated by the financial world and prefer to spend hours a day learning about asset classes, analyzing individual stocks, researching commodities futures, and even buying special data feeds for day-trading. Others would prefer to "set and forget" so that they can live their lives without having to keep an eye on the markets. You have to decide what level of effort you're willing to exert and whether or not you want to keep it up for the rest of your life. You may not want to work so hard when you're in your 80s, and your spouse may not want to take over a tricky stock portfolio if you're no longer able to make the decisions.

One aspect of risk is volatility, which greatly affects your investor psychology. Some abnormally calm retirees may be able to watch their portfolio drop 25% in a month while others can't sleep at night after a 2% drop. (No investor has ever complained about "upward volatility.") Logical financial analysis is worthless if your portfolio scares you or if your spouse is uncomfortable with the type of assets you're holding. See Appendix F on page 167 for more discussion about asset allocation.

If you're planning to work for a paycheck after you leave the military, your asset allocation should reflect the "human capital" that you're depositing on every payday. You can be much more aggressive with your investments when your spending money comes from paid employment. Pensions are the equivalent of another type of asset – the highest quality Treasury bills or I bonds. If you're receiving a pension (or if you're going to receive one later as Reservists/National Guard do at age 60), your other savings need to reflect that pension as a portion of the total assets. With a substantial portion of your assets in one of the world's best inflation-protected annuities, especially if it pays your expenses, then you can afford to put more of the rest of your assets into more aggressive equities. If you're ready to do this, be sure that you're also able to sleep at night.

ONE MILITARY couple began saving when they were junior officers and elected to keep over 90% of their investment portfolio in diversified equities. In October 1987, when the stock market dropped over 20% in a single day, they actually boosted their savings percentage to take advantage of the "sale." Years later, when the stock markets re-opened after the 9/11 attacks, they watched the value of their portfolio drop by over 40%. They stuck to their asset allocation, kept adding money during the market drop, and watched their portfolio recover over the next 18 months. As they contemplated their early-retirement plans, they realized that their experiences had given them the confidence to have a high tolerance for volatility. When they retired, one of them was receiving an active-duty pension and the other expected a Reserve pension in 20 years. Realizing the guaranteed value of their pensions, they elected to keep their portfolio over 90% in equities. Although they were withdrawing from their portfolio to pay their living expenses, if the stock markets dropped again they knew that they would be able to reduce their spending to a bare-bones budget. As they expected from their reading, their portfolio gains have also stayed well ahead of inflation.

By 2007 their portfolio had more than doubled as the market peaked. When the recession began late that year, their equities dropped in value by 40%, nearly wiping out six years of gains. Unlike the accumulation phase of working and investing, where paychecks and savings bought cheap stocks every month, it was painful for them to watch their retirement equities plunge in value. However, they took

continued

advantage of the slump to rebalance their asset allocation, to offset capital gains with capital losses, and to position their portfolio for the eventual recovery.

As they monitored their portfolio and their budget, they realized that despite the stock market's breathtaking volatility they had enough savings. There was more than enough to afford their lifestyle and they had plenty of room to cut spending if necessary. Websites and retirement calculators couldn't duplicate their experience of watching their portfolio plunge while they reconsidered their risk tolerance. They also discussed their feelings and decided that from now on they'd take a minor portion of the portfolio's dividends off the table each year.

MYTH #3: Worrying About Inflation

"You can't retire – inflation is too high!"

This is why you should consider maintaining a high percentage of your savings in equities. In over a century of data, they're the only asset class to beat inflation. Your pension has a COLA (and so does Social Security), but your personal rate of inflation may not match the official government CPI that determines the pension COLA. Keeping a significant portion of your assets in equities will give you both a hedge against inflation (your pension) and a weapon to beat it (your equities). See Appendix F on page 167 for a more detailed discussion.

MYTH #4: Making Savings Last

"Your savings need to be absolutely safe."

A huge investing epiphany for most military early retirees is realizing that their personal savings might not have to last forever. They may only need to cover the time they retire from the military until their additional pensions kick in from bridge careers, civil-service employment, or Social Security. Instead of choosing assets that may be eroded by inflation (like most bonds or certificates of deposit), early retirees may decide on a budget that includes consuming a portion of the portfolio before additional pensions (or Social Security) kick in. It may be worth the volatility risk to invest in higher-return assets (like small-cap value stocks, real estate trusts, or commodities) and liquidate a portion of the portfolio every year.

MYTH #5: Beating the Market

"Low-cost index funds are the way to go. Active investors can't beat the market."

"Warren Buffett beats the market every decade and we can too!"

"Why settle for average when you can pick a great active money manager?"

Few debates generate as much controversy as this one. The vast majority of investment managers never beat their fund's benchmark, but one or two of them have beaten it for at least 15 years. The vast majority of investors are also unable to beat the market, but investors like Warren Buffett continue to sublimely soar above the averages for decades. So who's right?

They're both right, and you have to decide which path you're going to pursue. You may have the innate skills of a Buffett, but like him you also have to be willing to make it your life. You may need to read a half-dozen newspapers a day and devour hundreds of financial reports a year while keeping in touch with dozens of business executives and investment managers. Do you find it absolutely fascinating, even compelling? Are you willing to put in at least 40 hours a week or longer in the pursuit of one needle among those haystacks of reports? Do you have Buffett's guts to "Be fearful when others are greedy and greedy when others are fearful?"

Maybe you're not Buffett (very few are) but you're confident that you can find the next Buffett. Or can you? Can you find the next hot fund manager for the next four or five decades? Can you sift through thousands of funds and make sure that they won't change their management or objectives after you invest with them? Are you willing to keep up with the research, the monitoring, and the workload for the rest of your life – or would you rather have a life?

You can beat the market if you're willing to work at it and if you can recover from your mistakes. For everyone else, there are low-cost passive index funds.

MYTH #6: Timing the Market

"I'm not touching the market right now. It's too expensive."

"I'm not touching the market right now. It's going down again and it won't recover for years."

"You have to invest with every paycheck, no matter how the market is doing, or your savings won't grow fast enough."

"I'm waiting until the Federal Reserve lowers the discount rate, the commodities futures index has stabilized, and the dollar strengthens against the yen."

Every one of these excuses may be a great reason not to invest for a retirement goal, but they're all excuses.

Research has found that the stock market rises approximately two-thirds of the time, largely in a random and unpredictable fashion. The stock market is not always driven by fundamental financial values, either; greed and hysteria are the common emotions, amplified by the media and investor psychology. Sitting on the sidelines waiting for the "perfect" moment is one of the biggest risks of all: the risk that inflation will erode the waiting cash and miss months or even years of compounding. While it is possible to time the market, it's nearly impossible to continue to time the market correctly through decades of retirement investing.

The vast majority of investors choose to add money to their retirement portfolio whenever they get it, which is usually with each paycheck. Some investors add the same amount every time (dollar-cost averaging or DCA), while others add more to their lagging investments and less to their strong performers (value-cost averaging). Every method has its advantages and drawbacks, but they all instill a discipline of routine investing that can be put largely on autopilot.

Ironically, DCA does not perform as well as "lump-sum" investing. For the best historical returns, all money should be invested as a lump sum on the first day it's available. But the reality is that this approach takes a cast-iron constitution approaching blind faith, and very few have the courage (or the blissful ignorance) to even consider attempting it. The real value of DCA is that it's a decision to make once and then automate with a checking-account deduction.

There are thousands of other investing myths, but by now the point has been made that there is no single best way to save for retirement. Each decision has both a financial and an emotional side, and each side has to agree before the decision will stand. Your supremely logical reasoning is also wasted if your partner can't tolerate the volatility or the other risks.

The best way to build the confidence to continue to save and invest under all circumstances is to educate yourself. Start with the Appendices plus the Recommended Reading books and websites, and keep reading until you find an approach that suits you. As you become more educated and experienced, your temperament will evolve to handle other types of investment strategies. You'll face the uncertainty with greater confidence, and you'll be able to ignore the market's short-term volatility to stay focused on your long-term goals.

Retirement Budgeting

The bad news is that retirement will involve a budget. The good news is that this budget is yours to refine, change, or even occasionally ignore. It can be as simple as the back of an envelope or as time-consuming as a multi-page spreadsheet. The whole point of **your** budget is to become comfortable with your spending predictions and to figure out how big your retirement investment portfolio will need to be for your financial independence.

Don't confuse a budget with a diet or an exercise program. Don't make it too ambitious, too confining, or too complicated. You're not trying to eliminate waste or to boost saving – those goals come later. At this stage you're only figuring out how much you're spending. Later you'll forecast your retirement expenses, and then you'll make your decisions about how long you'll have to keep earning paychecks. When you've finished with those steps, you can go back and tinker with your budget.

The first part of budgeting is easy: **track what you spend**. Don't clamp down on your spending, and especially don't criticize yourself or your family for wherever it's spent. Just start recording it in a logbook or a spreadsheet and figure out where it all goes. Generate your own system, download software, or save your receipts – whichever works best for you. The goal is to determine how much you're spending and to decide if your spending is aligned with your values.

Track your spending until you understand where you're spending your money. This may take only a month or two, or you may get in the habit of tracking your spending for decades (not a bad idea!). As you continue to track it, break your expenses down into meaningful categories. Again you can use pre-packaged software or come up with your own categories, but above all you should be able to distinguish between "essential" and "non-essential" spending. You'll also separate your categories into "pre-retirement" and "retirement" groups.

Retirement Finances

Everyone spends less in retirement, right? Not so fast.

It's true that you'll stop spending money on uniforms, commuting, childcare, and office expenses. If you're not driving as much, your vehicle insurance rates may drop. Your retirement income is taxed at a lower rate and might not be taxed at all by your state. Your lower income may put you in a smaller tax bracket, too. Your retirement tax bill will almost certainly be less.

But now the planning gets slightly more complex. You might be traveling more often, dining out several times a week, and spending more money on recreation. If you're relocating, your new home might have higher living expenses. You might decide to pay off the mortgage on your home, but if you move to a new area you may have a new mortgage. Now that you have the time, you might spend a lot more money on home improvement, landscaping, or hobbies. You may be able to cut back on your impulse purchases or do your own chores and maintenance, but you may need to spend more on supplies.

Make your best guess at your retirement budget. Read about your preferred retirement lifestyles, talk with your family and other retirees, and try to figure out your other preferences. Break your spending estimate down into essential and non-essential groups so that you have more flexibility. As you use this budget to calculate how much you'll need in your portfolio, you may decide to vary your spending or even to reduce some non-essential spending to reach your goal earlier. You have plenty of options, and the process will go through several iterations.

Once you have a retirement spending plan, you're ready to figure out how much it will cost. If you have enough assets to afford the plan, then you're all set! If not, you have a number of parameters and options to tinker with. One way or another you'll make this work.

How Much Will I Need?

The short answer: your retirement savings portfolio needs to be about 25 times the size of your net annual retirement spending. If you want to spend $40,000/year in retirement and you don't have any pension or other income, then you're going to need a million bucks in the bank. If you have a military pension, then your savings portfolio needs to be about 25 times the amount of your net annual retirement spending that's not already covered by your pension. If you have a $30,000 pension against your $40,000 retirement budget, then you only have to cover $10,000 and will only need $250,000 in savings.

The long answer comes from a number of research studies and retirement calculators. The oldest of them all, the Trinity study,[2] found that the most successful retirement portfolios survived for 30 years by starting at an annual "safe withdrawal rate" (SWR) of 4%. That initial SWR was raised each year by the rate of inflation (the CPI).

Twenty-five times annual spending may seem like a lot of money, and spending just 4% of your portfolio (plus inflation) seems simplistic. There are simply too many other variables. What if you have to put a new roof on the house or buy a new car? What happens to your spending if inflation soars or the stock market tanks? What if you live 40 or even 50 years in retirement?

But 25 times annual spending is a low number, too. It assumes that you'll consume the principal of your portfolio over the years and that you'll die broke. If you're concerned about living longer or if you don't want to touch the principal, you may need to save even more! Research indicates that retirees living off their stock dividends have saved as much as 33 times their annual spending.

So what's really the right number? Enter the calculators. There are dozens of different websites, programs, and spreadsheets. Most use historical data to predict the future, or sophisticated returns modeling, or detailed spending plans. Some take only a few minutes to enter data and run while others take hours of fiddling with inputs. The Recommended Reading section lists the most common approaches and the most popular applications.

Your retirement spending will fluctuate. Some retirees cut back in the first few years of retirement until they feel comfortable and confident enough to loosen the purse strings. Others embark on huge spending sprees as they enjoy fantasy vacations and home renovations. Locations and life-styles change with age. Some financial analysts even claim that retirement spending drops off dramatically when people reach their 80s, although their health care expenses may rise.

Most calculators do a poor job of estimating variations in retirement spending, and humans continue to make emotional decisions that calcula-tors can't predict. No matter how much money you have, you might find yourself traveling less if gas prices shoot up. If restaurants suddenly get more expensive, you might frequent cheaper places or eat out less. If the market tanks or the economy goes into recession, you may find it hard to plan for a fantasy vacation. You're probably already making conservative estimates of your spending, and if times seem tough then you'll probably defer non-essential expenses or even cut back on your lifestyle.

The spending estimate involves other assets, too. Military retirees may find that their pension (with its COLA) covers a substantial amount of their re-tirement expenses. Reservists and National Guard retirees will start a pen-sion (and health care) at age 60. You may be starting a bridge career or your spouse isn't ready to stop working yet. Despite the dire predictions of So-cial Security's insolvency, you'll have some form of this inflation-adjusted annuity. Depending on paychecks and pensions, your retirement spending may start out higher than 4% of your portfolio and drop over time.

How Much Can I Spend?

A 4% SWR is a starting point, one put forward over a decade ago and ap-pearing in print most frequently. It's straightforward, has a high success rate, and adjusts for inflation.

Researchers have proposed a number of alternatives. Some have pointed out that a high-equity portfolio can last for a longer time or survive a higher withdrawal rate. (High-equity portfolios can be very volatile but are a good counterbalance to a military pension.) Others have shown that if a retiree is willing to risk a slightly higher (yet still remote) possibility of failure, the SWR can be higher. One noted researcher, William Bernstein, even claims that planning for a higher success rate than 80% is unrealis-tic.[3] A higher standard would never have predicted the events of the 20th century, and it won't predict the events of the 21st.

Conservative portfolios (high in bonds and low in equities or other types of assets) can generally only support a lower SWR. Conservative retirement calculators recommend a lower SWR. Some researchers note that retiring into a declining stock market (like that of 2001-2002) leads to more failures than waiting until the market is recovering. Others have developed variable-spending systems of incredible complexity that permit higher initial SWRs but do not always adjust for inflation.

One author, Bob Clyatt, proposes a simple variable spending system.[4] Instead of the "4% plus inflation" of the Trinity study, Clyatt's system withdraws 4% every year. If the portfolio had a bad year and next year's 4% is smaller than 95% of the previous year's 4% withdrawal, then the retiree can take 95% of last year's withdrawal. The idea is that spending varies with portfolio performance and may have to be cut back during bad years. The safety net in Clyatt's system is that a retiree may also contemplate part-time work in bad years if spending can't be cut.

As always, military retirees have the benefits of a COLA-adjusted pension and much cheaper health care expenses. When coupled with a bridge career, part-time work, or a high-equity portfolio, these advantages will greatly improve portfolio survival through the economy's worst periods. The same benefits should provide a higher success rate in the future and may even allow a higher withdrawal rate. While the debate continues on several different Internet discussion boards, the consensus is that 4% is a starting point with many options for higher withdrawal rates.

Sample Calculations for a Warrant Officer Deciding When to Retire Under Final Pay

She joined the service in January 1980 (the Final Pay system) and was promoted to W-3 in January 2002.

A. After reaching time in rank in January 2005: The 2005 base pay for a W-3 with 24+ longevity years is $4,730.10/month and she has 25 years of service. Retired pay is $4,730.10 x 25 x 2.5% = $2,956/month.

B. After reaching a 26+ year longevity raise in January 2006 and retiring in November of that year: The 2006 base pay for a W-3 with 26+ longevity years is $5,032.50/month – the Final Pay system gives a retiree a 6% pay raise in just one year! Retired pay is $5,032.50 x [26 + 10/12] x 2.5% = $3,375/month. The pay raises plus an extra 22 months of service have raised retired pay by over 14%. Final Pay raises have an immediate impact on your retirement pay (unlike High Three raises) and are a compelling reason to verify your service entry date.

C. After an annual pay raise in January 2007: The 2007 base pay for a W-3 with 26+ longevity years is $5,143.20 – only a 2.2% raise. The extra two months of service don't make much of a difference, but the retired pay is $5,143.20 x 27 x 2.5% = $3,471/month.

D. After a targeted pay raise in April 2007: The April 2007 base pay for a W-3 with 26+ years has risen to $5,457 – another 6% raise just for hanging in there another four months. Again, the Final Pay system gives the full benefit of that raise for the rest of that W-3's life. Retired pay is $5,457 x [27 + 3/12] x 2.5% = $3,717/month – another 7% increase in retired pay and a full 25% over the January 2005 retirement.

Deciding When to Retire Under High Three

Veterans retiring under the military's High Three system use the average of the final 36 months of pay to determine their monthly pay used in their retirement calculation. This nearly eliminates the benefits of extending for longevity raises, annual pay raises, and any targeted pay raises.

After computing the average monthly pay, the High Three system uses the same service multiple as Final Pay.

Deciding Whether to Accept the
REDUX Career Status Bonus

This calculation is far more complicated than it seems. Read Appendix D on page 160 and then review the websites and articles listed on the Recommended Reading list, pages 185-186.

Short answer: Don't take the bonus. Retire under the High Three plan instead.

Long answer: Use a REDUX calculator to do the math for your situation. Unless you're staying for more than 20 years, it's probably not enough of a difference to take on the obligation and the risk.

The Department of Defense website shows that the REDUX Career Status Bonus (CSB) can produce more pension earnings than the High Three system. However, it assumes that the entire CSB (after taxes) is invested at a very optimistic rate of return (8% before taxes) and is saved for passing on to the veteran's heirs. Even with these liberal assumptions, the REDUX pension earnings don't pull ahead until the veteran is 75 years old. The payoff? $4,000 out of more than a million dollars.

For those who seek more detailed examples, the DoD website shows that most REDUX retirements lose out to their equivalent High Three retirement, even if the Career Status Bonus is invested. The sole clear REDUX winner is the E-9 retiring with 30 years of service. When using the REDUX calculator for your situation, consider using a lower rate of return from investing the Career Status Bonus. Even the E-9 example may not be a significant amount of money over the rest of a lifetime.

Whether or not you "know" that you'll be retiring after 25-30 years instead of 20 years, consider whether you're willing to risk the happiness of yourself and your family if your situation changes after the 15-year point. When you accept the CSB, you're essentially telling the assignment officer that you're willing to do anything, anywhere, anytime. You lose the flexibility of resigning before 20 years unless you pay back the CSB. More importantly, you lose the flexibility of leaving active duty for the Reserves or National Guard. The odds are probably in your favor, but this bet involves a risk of losing – one that you don't want to have to endure.

3

Start the Year Before

THE COUNTDOWN CHECKLIST that follows starts with the simplest case. It assumes that you're going to retire from active duty and that you have the financial independence to pursue different lifestyles with (at most) occasional part-time work.

Also before you dig too deeply into this chapter, let's assume that you've chosen the retirement date that optimizes your pension finances. Your service dates are correct for your retirement system, you're making the most of your rank's longevity pay raises, and, if necessary, you've stayed long enough for the latest pay raise.

Further, let's assume that you're not under long-term medical care. If you're facing a medical review board, many of this chapter's considerations will be on hold until the military decides whether you're retiring from active duty or transferring to the temporary disabled retired list. Although a medical retirement is more complex, it's probably in your best interests.

☐ Filing Your Retirement Request

Each service changes their deadlines and restrictions, but you'll want to file your retirement request up to a **year** ahead of your desired retirement date. This should allow ample time to meet all the notification requirements, to turn over to your relief, and to request an appropriate amount of terminal leave. Ideally, you've already attended your transition assistance course, but if not, this should be done as soon as you can get a date. Another advantage of such early notice is having ample time to complete any medical and dental care identified during the retirement physical.

Consider your terminal leave requirements very carefully. Depending on your duty location and your relocation plans, you could request up to 100 days of leave and permissive temporary duty. This would allow you to not only continue to draw your base pay but also all special pay and allowances. At the other end of your range of options, you could also choose to sell back the maximum amount of leave and remain on duty until the last possible minute; keep in mind that selling back leave only earns base pay without any special pay or allowances. The difference may require you to trade several months' additional labor (not leave!) for a cash boost to your retirement portfolio.

Once your chain of command has endorsed your retirement request, it's time to make the announcement you've been waiting for!

ONE VETERAN is very strongly motivated to plan his retirement down to the last detail because of his father's experience. Also a military veteran with more than 20 years of service, Dad hadn't realized that his first retirement check would arrive during the beginning of the **second** month of retirement. He hadn't saved enough money to cover the gap, and as a result the family had to vacate their base housing without enough money to provide for their next home. It was not a good way to start a new life. They spent several months in a tent at the local campground, saving pension checks to help them cover the deposits and rental for their next place.

☐ What to Tell Your Shipmates, Friends, Kids, and Parents

At first it may feel a little awkward (even embarrassing!) to talk about it. Military retirement can actually be a bit threatening to a veteran's identity. Your occupation may be a big part of who you are, and perhaps you feel like a valuable member of the team. You may have spent decades telling everyone, "I'm a Navy submariner." That approach works very well in fields that you don't actually have to retire from, such as law, medicine, or software. Even if you haven't earned any money in decades from those occupations, you're still what you do. Identifying with your avocation may not always be good, but it's certainly a ready-made response in our career-oriented society.

Try adding the "retired" word: "I'm a retired Air Force mechanic." That may be all the explanation required. Most civilians have little trouble believing that military retirees have earned their retirement and are entitled to do whatever they want. (Next you'll hear, "Congratulations, and thanks for your service!") Other veterans, however, seem to be our own worst enemy – "Yeah, yeah, I know that, you slacker, but what are you doing NOW?" You have to justify your existence.

Others may react quite differently. Retirees have a saying: "Your retirement will separate your friends from your co-workers." A true friend shares your hopes and dreams and will be happy for you when you achieve your goals. A co-worker may not appreciate your ambitions and may even feel that you're abandoning them to struggle with your old workload and to train your replacement. Even worse, some co-workers may seem jealous or frustrated that you're able to retire and they're not.

Many military people who are about to retire avoid discussing their plans with their co-workers. They'll talk about their leave and vacation plans without mentioning work. If pressed, they'll talk about going back to school, spending time with family, or even volunteering with charities. They share the details with their close friends but ask them not to spread the word until after they've retired.

Caution: your true shipmates and friends should share your joy at your success, but that doesn't mean they want to hear all the details ad nauseum. They may be humoring you while privately thinking that your plans aren't realistic. They may even think that you'll be looking for a job in a few months. (Refer back to Chapter 1's retirement "objections," page 11.) You might end up telling them that you just want to spend time with your family or to explore life for a while.

Unfortunately you'll have to play these situations by ear and by reading their facial expressions. Be cautious, be flexible, and don't be surprised by their reactions.

What about family members? If you're married, you and your spouse have already discussed and coordinated your plans. You've already shared all your information and reached an agreement. But how will your retirement affect your kids? Will they have to deal with yet another move? Will they worry that you don't have enough money? Will they understand the plan, or will they feel embarrassed to discuss it with you?

ONE VETERAN was finally ready for early retirement in the 1980s (the dawn of today's early retirement trend), but he felt that his daughter, a teenager, wasn't ready to handle the subject. In order to preserve the appearance of a normal home routine, he and his spouse pretended that he was still working – for several years! Each weekday he'd get up early, don "office attire," load up his briefcase, and leave the house while his daughter was getting ready for school. After she was out of the house he'd return to resume his secret life as a trailblazing early retiree.

Years later his daughter was married with kids of her own. One day he confessed to his subterfuge and asked her how she would have handled the knowledge that he'd retired so early while all her other friends' parents were still working. Once she got over her surprise, she couldn't help laughing at his concern. She said that she was far too busy dealing with all of the problems of being a teenager, and even if she had noticed that he was retired she wouldn't have cared as long as it didn't affect her life.

Younger kids (up to school age) may not fully understand the idea of retirement. You've probably been working for their whole life and they may not know anyone who's retired. At their age it's best to stick to the big picture. They want to know that you'll be spending time with them and they might care that you have enough money in the budget for some fun. Once they realize that you're not deploying any more, they'll happily skip the details!

Adolescents may be a bit more concerned. They know that people have jobs to pay the bills, and they want to know where their allowance is coming from. It's a good idea to allocate plenty of time to talk about it, to answer all their questions, and to let them know that you're going to be able to spend more time with them. You may be earning less money than during your working days, but you have a budget that includes everyone's needs. You may have to have this conversation several times over weeks or even months – they may be a little skeptical and seek reassurance. (They're also talking it over with their friends, who are reporting this news to the other parents.) Once your kids are assured that you can coach their team or chaperone their school field trips, they'll be just as enthusiastic about retirement as you are.

Teenagers can be a tough sell. While they're figuring out their own identity and taking their first steps to independence, they just want their parents to be normal, invisible, and available. Parental non-conformance is embarrassing enough, and they're not necessarily going to be enthusiastic about all the time you'll want to spend with them! At this age you may have to discuss the family budget at length and make sure everyone understands the changes. Your pension may even seem like a lot of money to them (especially if they want a car), and they may not appreciate that it has to last you for the rest of your life. If the family is going to be moving away from their school and their friends, you'd better have a good justification for this "disaster." If you want your teens to support your retirement, you'll have to show them how it's going to improve their life. Good luck with that – maybe you don't want to move until after they've finished high school.

Your parents (and your in-laws!) might be even a tougher sell than your teens. In fact their reaction to your announcement might make you feel like a rebellious teen again. They know all your flaws and weaknesses, and, although they might be proud of your accomplishments, they won't hesitate to question your judgment. (From their perspective, your spendthrift indolence might put their loved ones on the streets.) If your parents have retired, then you should be able to reassure them – especially if you ask for their advice.

If your parents are still working, however, you can expect to encounter resistance. If they have avocations of their own or feel that they'll never save enough to retire, then you will have difficulty explaining yourself. You and your spouse will have many "interesting" discussions with them as they attempt to reconcile their standards with yours. The best approach is to emphasize the time you'll be able to spend with family (including them and their grandchildren) and to talk about taking a few years off to explore life. Much later they may accept your decision, although privately they may despair that you'll ever be able to hold down a real job again.

□ Choosing Where to Live

This is only one of your retirement decisions, but it needs a **lot** of preparation. Start early – even a year may leave you wishing that you had more time for your research.

Consider the typical military mindset. After 20 or more years of travel, many deployments, and a dozen moves (perhaps with a growing family), you've learned that you can set up housekeeping in record time. You may even be able to arrive in town on a Friday and by the following week have a place to live, put the kids in school, and report to your new duty station.

When you retire, it's tempting to simply fall back on those skills one last time. It's easy to find a new town and quickly set up a new life – although this time **you're** in charge of all the decisions. The biggest difference, though, is that this new life may be for the rest of your lives!

The family discussions that led you to retirement will help you again when you decide where you're going to live. (Yes, this time it should be a group decision, and you may end up with a minority vote.) This time it's not even about you or your immediate family, but also your extended family and your preferences. Do you want to live near your siblings and cousins? Are your parents likely to need your support with medical issues or home maintenance or even full-time care? Or would you rather choose your own lifestyle, climate, and location while accepting that you may have to travel to visit your extended family?

Take your time. After decades of making quick decisions, there's no need to rush to make this one. Learn the latest rules on base housing and storing/moving your household goods, and use those benefits as much as possible. You may have to vacate your base housing after you retire, and you may only have a year to decide where to move your possessions, but you can take years to decide on your eventual retirement location. It's only a matter of what issues you (and your family) are confronting and how many times you want to move.

There are many books, websites, and periodicals to help you decide exactly where you want to live and whether you want to purchase or rent a place. Take advantage of those resources very early in your retirement planning. Read about towns you are interested in on the Internet and, if you zero in on a specific location, subscribe to the town's newspaper. Ask the local Chamber of Commerce for more information or (if possible) look up old friends, shipmates, and relatives. Join an Internet discussion board in that area and ask for advice. Gather all the information you can, discuss it with your family, and make sure that you still want to move there. You may decide to change your mind more than once.

After you arrive at your chosen destination, don't rush to set up your new life. There's no need to buy a house that weekend or even to put the kids in school right away. This is a great time to rent for a while and to learn the local real estate market. While you may know the area, now you'll have to take time to reacquaint yourself with the details. Is the old neighborhood still a great place to raise a family, or is it looking a little run-down? How has traffic changed over the years? What new roads or neighborhoods will be built over the next decade? Are there any issues with electricity, water, sewage, schools, or zoning? What activities do you and your family enjoy, and how close do you want to be to them?

☐ How Far Away From the Commissary, Medical, Dental?

In establishing your new life, you also need to keep in mind your veteran's benefits. Although the savings of exchanges and commissaries are always under pressure from multinational stores and big-box chains, you may still prefer their selection and pricing. Although you can choose many different levels of TRICARE health insurance, you may want to be near a major military medical facility. If you or a loved one have a chronic health condition, you may not want to spend hours driving hundreds of miles every month.

When you consider your new life, you'll have to shop around for more than a home. Sample the selection and pricing in the local stores. If you're in an area with several military bases, sample them all. For example, the Army might have a better exchange than the Navy exchanges you've always patronized, or it might be closer to home.

ONE FAMILY happily retired in Hawaii – sunshine, beaches, and surfing! However, even a relatively small move ended up having large consequences.

Their first decision was health care and infrastructure. Although it seemed attractive and cheaper to live on a neighboring island, or far away from Honolulu and other big towns, they realized that their lifestyle depended on ready access to health care and home-improvement supplies. Although the neighboring islands were improving, Oahu still offered the most experienced doctors as well as the best selection of merchandise and prices.

The first surprise was shopping. They had always used the naval base's exchange/commissary because they were convenient to work. Now that they weren't working, it was much easier to shop at the army base just a few miles up the highway. Then they discovered that Costco and Wal-Mart frequently had better prices on many items, so they learned to keep track of the sales and other bulk-purchase opportunities.

While they had expected to send their children to a private school near the naval base, they later chose to stay with their neighborhood public school. They avoided a rush-hour commute (30 minutes each way) for a school with the same quality and no private tuition fees. Neighbors and playmates were involved with the same school which brought everyone closer together. They also lived close enough for their kids to bicycle or walk to school, greatly improving everyone's convenience and independence.

☐ Military-Friendly States

During your career you've probably been a resident of a state that doesn't tax their active-duty military or at least gives you a big tax break on your income. That's going to change!

Taxes are one of the minor reasons for choosing your retirement location, but they will affect your retirement budget. While you're discussing climate, family, and lifestyle, you should also consider how much you'll have to pay for the privilege of your chosen location.

Most states do not tax disability retired pay, and several states do not tax military pensions. The rules are always changing (Ohio recently stopped taxing military pensions) and the details may have more impact than you appreciate. You'll also want to consider the cost of sales tax, property tax, asset taxes, taxes on investment income, and even county/city taxes. Registering your vehicles in your new state may require hefty fees and taxes.

If you're planning to continue your education or if you have kids in high school, there's another factor to consider in choosing your state residence: tuition rates. Several state colleges offer reduced tuition to residents and may even offer scholarships for you or your family. Other state schools may reduce their tuition for even minor veteran's disability ratings.

If you've decided on a civil-service bridge career, you may choose to work for a state's civil service instead of the federal government. The state may offer hiring preference to veterans (especially with a disability rating) and other benefits for you and your family.

While you shouldn't choose your retirement residence solely for its tax advantages, it can make a difference in your retirement budget and thus your quality of life. If you're unhappy about paying thousands of dollars a year in property taxes, you may want to cross a state line in search of a similar lifestyle. If your retirement plans take you near a state line, then consider the tax situation on both sides before making your decision.

Read Early-Retirement.org's "FAQ Archives" for more resources to research tax-friendly states.

☐ Are You a Perpetual Traveler?

After decades of changing duty stations, maybe you don't want to tie yourself down to one location!

One of the biggest interests of retirees is travel – seeing the world at your own pace and without a set of orders. Perpetual travelers (PTs) stay weeks or even months in a location, or travel with a motor home. Campgrounds are certainly a cheaper way to stay, but options include discount vacation rental condominiums, trailer parks, or house sitting. Recreational vehicles are by far the most popular travel mode, but other retirees wait patiently for hops on military flights.

A surprisingly frugal retirement lifestyle is living aboard a boat. Particularly near the Intracoastal Waterway along the Atlantic and Gulf coasts of the U.S., large groups of boaters move north during summers (away from hurricane season) and south during winters. Others head for the open ocean on both coasts.

Even families can adopt a perpetual-traveler lifestyle. Although the recreational vehicle or boating life is easiest for adults, a few families make it work through homeschooling or only summer travel. If yours is the type of family who's always enjoyed a boating or outdoor lifestyle, this may work for you.

Technology has dramatically improved the logistics of perpetual travel. With cell phones, mobile Internet access, and overnight shipping, the PT lifestyle has never been easier. Bills can be paid electronically or through automatic debit. Traditional mail-forwarding services will send your paper to your next port call. Other companies will actually open your mail, scan the contents, and post the images to a website for you to peruse at your leisure. Banks, stock brokerages, and other regulated financial institutions may require a more permanent address than a post office box or a mail-forwarding service, but PTs also use the mailing address of friends or families and conduct their business online. If you're planning to keep a current driver's license and pay your taxes, you will also need to claim residency in a state. The amount of time you spend in other states during your travel may also render you susceptible to that state's income taxes. However, these and other challenges have already been faced by thousands of PTs and successfully worked out.

See the Recommended Reading section on page 181 for more information, especially the books and website of Billy and Akaisha Kaderli.

☐ The Expatriate Lifestyle: Intriguing But Not for Everyone

A significant minority of retirees have noted that their financial portfolios won't support their lifestyles in Manhattan or Los Angeles, but are more than adequate for expenses in Mexico or Bangkok.

The most famous overseas early retirees are Paul and Vicki Terhorst and Billy and Akaisha Kaderli. They've been traveling the world since 1984 and 1989 respectively and show no signs of stopping. After two decades of travel through Europe, Asia, and South America, the Ter-horsts built a home in a rural area outside Buenos Aires but continue visiting their favorite places. The Kaderlis have spent most of their time in Southeast Asia and Mexico, but have been to many other coun-tries. They maintain a small home in a U.S. resort community, but they spend the majority of their time abroad.[1, 2]

You may have seen some of the expatriate lifestyle on overseas duty or during port calls, but now you can live it full time. Both couples, as well as many other retirees, have learned that expat living offers a chance to get to see the "real" country and to know its people. Instead of staying in resorts and hotels, they rent city apartments, shop at local stores, eat at local restaurants, and blend into the community. "Going local" means learning to speak the language and cook the cuisine, cel-ebrating that culture's holidays, understanding how to get around by public transportation, and knowing where to do the laundry.

Once again modern technology has made the expat lifestyle easier than ever before. Many overseas cell phones are actually more common, more fully featured, yet less expensive than those in the U.S. Cheap Internet access is widespread in metropolitan areas and most rural ones. Modern clothing fabrics and compact toiletries mean that luggage can be reduced to a roller bag and a backpack. Most finances can be handled through ATMs and the Internet. A dropping dollar may raise prices for expatriate Americans, but plenty of bargains can still be found by staying for weeks or months in an area and really getting to know the local culture. If the dollar rises, then expat purchasing power just went up with it.

Expat retirees rarely become overseas citizens or residents. Instead of navigating the bureaucracy (and perhaps paying double taxes) they re-quest long-term tourist visas or "restart the clock" by leaving the coun-try for brief periods. TRICARE is not easily accessible overseas (ex-cept when space is available at U.S. military medical facilities), but you may pay less out of pocket or even purchase your own catastrophic-care policy. It's possible to find work (for example, teaching English or pro-viding services over the Internet or consulting), but earned income will subject you to taxation by both your host country and possibly the U.S. As a U.S. citizen you are still expected to pay U.S. taxes and maintain a state residence address.

Don't despair if you have a family. Just like perpetual travelers, many families have found a way to let the world be both their residence and their school system. If your kids have put up with your changing duty stations, they'll easily adapt to the overseas lifestyle and be far worldlier than their domestic cousins.

The perpetual-traveler and expatriate lifestyles aren't as difficult as they appear, and technology provides a wealth of solutions. You don't have to be a trailblazer or even a rugged pioneer, and you can travel the world at your own pace. However, the details of both lifestyles are far beyond the scope of this book. More references are in the Recommended Reading section, page 181.

4

Countdown to Your Final Six Months

I DEALLY, BY SIX MONTHS before retirement the big decisions have been made. The rest is "just" a matter of executing your plans and handling the surprises. Before you start into the checklist details, take a moment to review your progress.

By now you and your family have gone over the complicated issues. While there may not be perfectly harmonious agreement, you've probably made a decision to retire and another decision about a bridge career. You've reviewed your finances and discussed where you want to live. You've filed the request and made sure that it's being processed. Your relatives, shipmates, co-workers, and friends are all aware that you're retiring and everyone has dealt with their initial reactions. By now any family or command resistance should at least be grudging acceptance (if not cheerful cooperation) and everyone's making appropriate plans.

☐ Attending the Transition Assistance Programs (TAP) Training

A year or two ago, when you first started thinking about retirement, you would have attended your service's training on transition assistance planning. (The retirees are laughing about this suggestion.) The reality is that it's hard to schedule time away from the mission when you haven't even made a retirement decision. You might be reluctant to tip your hand by going to TAP when you're supposed to be a hard-charging leader, and most commands don't really make time for your absence until you've already requested retirement. Thus, we'll start this chapter with a review of the contributions that TAP can make to your retirement checklist.

Whether you're seeking a bridge career or planning to be a surfer bum, the Department of Defense wants to ensure that you understand your benefits and are aware of their timing. (No one wants to see veterans sleeping under highway overpasses or standing in line at the food bank.) You're going to be stuck at TAP until the instructors are satisfied that you've been "trained." The briefings may be fascinating, but they could also cover topics that you are already familiar with, so bring plenty of material to keep yourself entertained while you're waiting for new information to come up. Even if you're offered the opportunity to complete your review online instead of in person, it might be better to plant yourself in a conference room with fellow TAP or make the most of your "us time" – try to coordinate your schedule with your spouse's and attend TAP together. Even if you two have already made the important decisions, one of you is sure to notice a detail that's been overlooked. You'd much rather have your spouse at TAP to talk about the briefs than to try to go over it later from your notes, and you'll both feel more comfortable going through the process together. If your spouse isn't completely on board, TAP will go a long way toward settling your differences.

While you're at TAP, be alert for any mention of tasks that need to be completed before you're formally retired. You'll have a generic checklist, but you'll have to modify it for your situation and your schedule. As inconvenient or even painful as some checklist items may appear to be on your last day at the command, they'll be extraordinarily more difficult after you're a retiree. Some retiree updates and corrections may take months to be processed if you're no longer on active duty. Others just can't be done, even if you're willing to pay the expenses.

TAP HELD NO surprises for one veteran who'd been preparing to retire early for years, but it was a rude awakening for some of her fellow TAP attendees. During the pay brief, it gradually dawned on the class that their last active-duty pay would be deposited at the end of the month before they retired, and that it would be at least a month before they saw their first retirement deposit. No one was happy to hear the instructor suggest that retirees should have two months' expenses in cash in case the pay branch had a glitch in the retirement paperwork. The facial expressions and muttered comments made it clear that this was an unpleasant contingency that would change the timing of a number of bridge-career plans.

At an absolute minimum, spend your free TAP moments reviewing your service record and medical/dental records. Make sure that all of your reports or evaluations are present and that the dates cover all of your service. Verify that your medical/dental records contain every health concern that you may be taking into retirement, and make a list of questions to discuss during your exams. If your issues aren't addressed before you retire, you may have to start all over again with the Veteran's Administration.

☐ Self-Assessment Software and Worksheets

If you haven't made a decision about a bridge career, TAP is a good place to research the question. The curriculum and the training aids are all designed to help you identify a field and find a job that meets your criteria. The instructors will be very familiar with the self-assessment tools, and they'll also be able to discuss a job search. Just talking about the process may convince you that it's not as difficult as it seems – or you may decide that employment is definitely not in your future.

Once you've squared away your records, take the time to explore the self-assessment programs and documents. Even if you're convinced that you'll never work again, you may be surprised by the wealth of knowledge you'll gain from the personality and temperament surveys. The interest questionnaires can also help you decide how you feel about perpetual travel, moving to a new area, volunteer work, and new hobbies. Talk to the staff about your concerns and tailor the resources to your needs. This may be the last time for months that you can reflect in quiet exploration and contemplation.

If you're attending TAP with your spouse, try to take the assessments and surveys together. The results may surprise you – in a good way! Even if the TAP schedule doesn't have the time, you may want to revisit these tools to help make sure that you're both in sync with your retirement plans.

☐ Discharge Paperwork

Each service processes discharge and separation forms (DD-214's) with their own specific procedures, but try to review your rough draft as early as six months before you retire.

The DD-214 is the official summary of where you've served and what you've done. If there's a special skill or qualification that you feel is important to your future benefits or your resume, then make sure it's on your DD-214 – or make sure you understand why it can't be done. It's hypothetically possible to correct an error after you've retired, but it's also a lengthy bureaucratic experience that may ultimately fail. You've spent years of training to get it right the first time, and the DD-214 is one of the most important places to make that happen.

After retirement, most veterans stuff their DD-214 into an "important papers" file and forget about it. This almost guarantees that it will be missing the next time you need it. Make several copies and include them with all your important papers: your copy of your service record, your medical records, and your financial records. You'll even want to include a copy with your will. Scan an encrypted copy onto your hard drive or upload it to a file-saving website. Archive another copy with a retiree organization. If possible, register your DD-214 with the county clerk's office where you settle after retirement. In most places, you'll get back a certified copy for your own use. More importantly, your DD-214 can then be retrieved by your properly designated representatives (executor, spouse, children). You won't have to go looking for it when you apply for veterans' exemptions on real-estate taxes or other post-retirement benefits that might be available where you live.[1] You, your executor, and your family will be glad you did.

A NUCLEAR engineering officer reviewed the draft of his DD-214 and realized that there was nothing on the record to indicate that he had served in nuclear engineering billets. The personnel office explained that the proper codes were not on the officer's record and thus could not be added to the DD-214. His research determined that the appropriate branch of the Navy's Bureau of Personnel did not add these codes for billets held less than a year due only to the available space on reports. When he explained his concerns to their office, BUPERS agreed to add the codes to his record so that they could be added to his DD-214. The research, official request, and eventual update to the DD-214 took more than two months.

☐ Medical and Dental Exams

Next time you're chatting with a bunch of veterans, ask them how their discharge physicals went – and listen to their groans of pain. But, seriously, take a few minutes to ask these people what they wish they'd done differently during their physicals. Heed their advice and don't repeat their oversights!

The Department of Defense performs your physical to make sure that you're healthy and that you receive appropriate medical treatment before you're discharged. It's their legal due diligence to prove that they took care of you before you left active duty. You, on the other hand, need to make sure that you understand every aspect of your physical condition and correct as many things as possible during active duty before you have to do it through the Veteran's Administration or TRICARE. It's the same idea as a DD-214: get it right the first time or spend months of retirement trying to do it on your own.

When you fill out the paperwork for your physical and start your exams, you or the medical staff may discover new questions or old unresolved issues. Some can be handled immediately, but others may require additional time and testing. It's quite possible to need several months to chase down all the consultations with other doctors, to schedule the complicated examinations like MRIs or CAT scans, and to make a final assessment of the condition/treatment. It's an unpleasant process, but it's even more excruciating if you delay.

Prepare yourself **before** you make your first appointment. Read your entire medical record from start to finish and go all the way back to your entrance exam. Make sure you understand every entry, especially any conditions or injuries or illnesses that may follow you into retirement. If you don't understand the entries, research the vocabulary on the Internet or ask your shipmates. If you have a health-related problem while in uniform, you can confidently assume that it could develop into an even bigger problem in retirement. Make a list of your issues and questions and be ready to discuss them with technicians, medical staff, and doctors.

When you're completing the physical's tests and exams, make sure that you understand everything added to your record. If something doesn't look right, or if it isn't thoroughly explained to you, then there's a problem. An innocuous oversight now may miss an existing condition that could grow worse during your retirement, or it could even result in the denial of a disability claim.

It's quite likely that you'll leave the exam with a list of consultations, extra appointments, and more testing. Researching the issues and evaluating your treatment options could take a serious chunk out of your final few months. If you start early, you'll have time to handle the inevitable delays, seek other opinions, and make thoughtful decisions.

Even if all of your questions were answered during the exams and tests, ask your doctor again during the final exam. Bring your list, work it all the way through, take good notes, and don't get put off or distracted. If your doctor doesn't seem to have the time for you, ask for another appointment – or another doctor! No one can take more care than you to make sure that your exam information is correct, that all issues have been examined, and that you're in the best possible condition before you retire. I can't stress strongly enough how important it is to chase down these nagging questions **before** you complete the physical and retire.

If you're fortunate enough to be attached to a command with its own independent-duty medical staff, give them an extra-nice favor in exchange for a review of your discharge physical. You might not recognize an incomplete entry or a missing signature, but they'll know what to look for. This can help avoid delays during your final checkout or if you ever have your records screened by the Veteran's Administration health care system.

Determining disability ratings and dealing with the Veteran's Administration are far beyond the scope of this book. If your separation physical discovers a condition that may lead to extensive medical care or even disability concerns, then seek professional help from the medical facility. You may even need to review your rights with your military legal staff. What seems to be a straightforward retirement may become mired in months of medical evaluation boards, disability rating reviews, and maybe even time on the Temporary Disabled Retired List. No one wants this disruption during the planning for the next phase of their life, but you have decades in front of you and the process may be worth tens of thousands of dollars in medical benefits. The person who you'll become in 30 or 40 years will be heartily glad that you persevered.

Prescriptions are an aspect of your retirement life that may require considerable thought and planning. Your prescription costs will be considerably cheaper than those of civilian retirees, but you'll still need to make sure you can get what you want, in sufficient quantity, when you want it. Consider where you'll be retired, whether the standard pharmaceutical formulary meets your medication needs, and whether or not you can obtain your medications through TRICARE's mail-order pharmacy. These questions should be asked during your first medical screening, not during the final physical exam. Discuss the treatment/medication choices with your doctor, and then have a long talk with the head of the pharmacy department. Once you've all decided on a long-term medication plan, stock up as much as you can before you retire. You don't want to run low on your 30-day supply only to find out that there's been a glitch with transferring your access to the retiree prescription system. Give yourself plenty of time to work through the procedures and, if necessary, to figure out another solution before you run out or have to pay out of your own pocket. This even applies to routine medications such as allergy pills or birth control.

Fully exploit your active-duty or Reserve benefits **before** you retire. If you've been planning to stop smoking, lose weight, or deal with some other medical/lifestyle aspect, start that project while you're still on active duty. Depending on your personal/family situation and how much you enjoy planning your life, you may even decide to complete a final pregnancy or vasectomy or tubal ligation with the military health care system. If you're moving from a large military medical system with outstanding care to a remote retirement location with less than excellent facilities, this may be an important decision.

Your retirement physical includes a dental exam. Make the most of it, because retirement dental insurance can be expensive. Consider doing a full set of x-rays, get a good cleaning, and check the condition of any fillings or other dental issues. Once you retire you may be fortunate enough to only need an exam every 18-24 months, and it's frequently cheaper to negotiate a discount with your dentist than to pay for insurance.

VETERAN'S STORY: Before one veteran became an early retiree, he was honorably discharged with a service-connected disability from an injured shoulder and a fractured skull. It was in his best interest to educate himself about the discharge process, so he researched the references and insisted on a medical evaluation. The thorough evaluation of the injuries, as well as their documentation in his medical records, was critical to dealing with the Veteran's Administration after discharge. Twenty years later he had the first of several shoulder replacements. Although the evaluation seemed like a huge bureaucratic hassle at the time, it guaranteed his benefits and saved thousands of dollars.

OFFICER'S STORY: An officer was being retired under the 1990s Temporary Early Retirement Authority, which meant that she was leaving with less than 20 years of service and a substantial reduction in her pension. She was unhappy and frustrated before she started her discharge physical, so she was even more annoyed by the time-consuming EKGs and several other repeated cardiac tests. The doctors were finally able to rule out equipment problems, though, and they delivered the news that she'd developed a heart murmur from a leaky valve. Her retirement was put on hold for open-heart surgery, two months of rehabilitation, and several years on the Temporary Disabled Retired List. She doesn't recommend this retirement technique for others, but her perseverance saved her life, ensured that she'd be able to enjoy it with her family, and incidentally earned her more pension and disability income.

NON-COMMISSIONED STORY: A senior non-commissioned officer was retiring in four months, so he reluctantly started his command's retirement checkout sheet. His foot-dragging was due to what he had decided would be a painful experience: the dental clinic. Sure enough, his usual neglect had caused several new problems. The difference this time, though, was that the dentists refused to complete their portion of his retirement checklist until he'd completed his treatment. It took every bit of those four months to finish eight root canals, including problems that should have been addressed years ago. His was probably one of the military's most painful outpatient retirement transitions.

☐ Exit Interviews and Last-Minute Questions

You've been waiting years for this exit interview! All of your weapons are ready to fire, the missiles are ready for launch, and you have tons of bombs to drop. You've been holding back far too long and the military can't possibly survive without your opinion of what's broken, who should be fired, and how to fix everything.

Get that attitude well out of your system before you sit down with your chain of command. Be classy – don't be rude or crass. Although exit interviews are a great opportunity to tell your bosses and co-workers what you really think of them as you exit the smoking rubble, you don't want to be remembered for this poor behavior. It's doubtful that you'll make anything better by hurling these hand grenades as you leave, and you certainly don't want to make things worse than they already are for your friends and co-workers. Besides, why were you saving it for the exit interview? Talking trash is also a confession that you were unwilling to deal with the issues when you were working with these people. Focus on your new life, not your old scores.

Focus your exit interview on the command's accomplishments and on what helped you succeed. If your bosses are doing a good job, they need to know that their work is appreciated. Emphasize that anyone can do your job, especially your relief, if they have the right tools and if they're set up to succeed. You might even want to talk about where the current projects could go or what other challenges should be tackled.

Be happy about your new life, but don't go over the top. As you approach retirement you may be surprised to hear about it from a number of jealous bosses and co-workers. Self-centered people won't celebrate your retirement; they'll feel sorry or envious that it's not theirs. They won't compliment you or ask what you're going to do the first day of your retirement. Instead, they'll say that they wish they knew how to invest like you did. Even worse, your boss may decide that you're making a serious mistake and might spend the entire exit interview trying one more time to "fix you" before it's too late. Share your plans but don't feel that you have to justify them or account for your time. Agree to consider everyone's helpful suggestions after you've taken a little time off.

Before you start your exit interviews, decide how you're going to respond to the following questions:

- Can you stay a couple days/weeks/months longer?

- After you leave, where can we reach you with questions?

- Can you come in for lunch next week?

- Can you help us find a volunteer to...?

- We know you're retiring, but can you to come in to take care of...?

- Hey, you'll have plenty of time on your hands! Can you help us with...?

Of course once you're out of the command, there's nothing holding you back from blowing the whistle to higher authority. Hold off a few weeks before taking this step, however, because the whole issue may seem trivial with some rest and a new retirement perspective. If it wasn't a problem worth addressing when you were attached to that command, then it's probably not worth your time after you've left it.

☐ Cleaning Up the Details

Over the years you've depended on your base's legal office to take care of your wills, medical directives, powers of attorney, and other important family documents. Your retirement may involve moving to another state (or even another country!), finding new doctors and dentists, selling and buying real estate, and changing many other aspects of your life. Review your legal files and update these documents before you leave the command.

As you complete your command's checklist and review your pay statements, make sure all your travel claims have been paid and that your government credit card is turned in. The Defense Finance and Accounting Service audits your final pay record and will eventually correct any oversights, but this could take up to a year.

While you're planning your retirement timeline, pay close attention to your leave balance. Remember that you'll continue to accrue leave at the rate of 2½ days per month right up until the day you retire, and that leave either has to be used or sold back. If you're moving to a new location after you retire, you may be eligible to take permissive temporary duty in addition to using your leave. If your leave balance is exceptionally high after a deployment, you may have to use some of it to avoid losing it at the end of the fiscal year! The rules vary for each service and deployment situation. Research your service and command policies to determine how you'll use your leave and then schedule it around your other retirement actions.

The military only considers a day of leave to be worth a day of base pay – no allowances or special pays. If you decide to sell back a month of leave, then you'll get exactly one month of base pay and no more. While that's quite a bit of money to start your retirement with, it might make more sense to delay your retirement date to enjoy an entire month of leave while collecting not only base pay but all of your other entitlements. You have to decide whether time or money is more important to you, as well as the risk of your command recalling you while you're "just" on leave.

If you decide to sell back leave, make sure that taxes are either withheld from your lump sum or that you pay estimated taxes on the amount. If you don't have sufficient tax withheld from your pay (including your sold leave) during the year, you'll encounter late-payment penalties and interest charges on your tax return.

While you're reviewing your pay statement, consider maximizing your contributions to the Thrift Savings Plan. Whether you're separating or retiring, you have one final opportunity to boost your account in the world's largest and cheapest investment funds. As of this writing, the TSP funds charge an expense ratio of 0.03% (only three basis points!), and veterans may even be eligible to roll their IRA over to their TSP account. These are once-in-a-career decisions that will affect years of tax-deferred compounding. Review the TSP rules, talk with your command's TSP representative, and make the decision well before your retirement ceremony.

Whether you plan to start a bridge career or become a diehard surf bum, consider whether you want to maintain your security clearance. Your command security manager will have the appropriate statement to put in your civilian resume to refer to your military clearance.

Give your DD-214 one more check before you detach from the command. The personnel staff may not release your final copy until your retirement date, or they may be able to forward it to your new address.

Back at work, inventory all the gear that your job is entitled to and make sure that the gear you're responsible for is actually present or accounted for. Wherever possible, make sure that it's under your personal control or locked away or transferred to someone else's custody. The person intending to take over your job may balk at doing so until they have the tools they need. If something isn't where it's supposed to be, then either find it right now or else stiffen your resolve and start the investigation. It's hard to imagine a worse way to spend the week before retirement than looking for "missing" objects.

Speaking of missing objects, hang onto your receipts for turning in any classified material you used to possess. The command may not discover any "issues" until weeks or even months after you retire, and your receipt is the only proof that you didn't lose anything. The command may also appreciate your assistance with clearing up any problems in their own records, and your receipts will be a big help to the investigating officer.

It goes without saying that you should also return any "borrowed" office equipment or supplies. While they may have eased your military burden through telecommuting or the road warrior life, they're not yours to take into retirement. After years of squeezing your command's budget and pinching pennies, you may be surprised to learn that pens, paper, and other office equipment are surprisingly affordable at many fine retail outlets. Make a fresh start on your retirement by using anything more stylish than government-furnished office supplies.

While you're dreaming about a fresh start, are you already living in your retirement location or will you need to move? If you're moving, when do you want to do that? Depending on your housing situation, you may be able to extend your stay until after your retirement. Although you may be eager to start your new life after the military, the last few months before retirement will be a very hectic time. You'll be wrapping up the loose ends at work, putting the finishing touches on your retirement ceremony, and gathering all your family and friends. You'll probably have a number of house guests over the next few weeks, and that's a very difficult time to start sorting possessions for packing or storage.

If command operations and your retirement timeline permit it, try to have your retirement ceremony at least a week before you start packing out your household goods. That'll give you time to finish detaching from your command, send off your last house guests, clean up after their departure, and have some time to catch your breath before you start preparing for the move. It'll also give you a chance to figure out what you're going to do with all those retirement presents and plaques!

☐ The Retirement Ceremony

Some of you have been waiting for decades and you've planned every minute of the event. Enjoy yourselves! You know what you want to do.

Perhaps some of you are retiring unexpectedly, or at least you haven't thought much about your ceremony. Maybe you feel that the command owes you their appropriate recognition and validation for all your years of sacrifice, and you'd like as much ceremony as you're entitled to. If that's the case, then please talk about your ceremony with your command as soon as your request has been approved. A command can't be expected to figure out what every member wants included in their ceremony, and a number of honors may take weeks or even months to arrange, especially if they're signed by an elected official or a celebrity.

A very small minority of you may not want any ceremony at all. That's your privilege, but you may encounter significant resistance. Your command wants you to have a fair opportunity to enjoy a ceremony without intimidation or coercion. Your bosses, who have probably thought about their own retirement ceremonies occasionally, may have a hard time believing that you don't share their enthusiasm for pomp and protocol. They may feel that you're mistakenly passing up the opportunity to celebrate your achievements and to bring closure to a long, distinguished career. Some commands (you know the type) may be concerned that you'll change your mind about the ceremony and blame the military for not accommodating your desires. They don't want bitter retirees starting Congressional inquiries!

If you'd prefer to avoid a retirement ceremony, it's best to express that sentiment early and often. Some cite personal reasons while others prefer to avoid the extensive time, effort, and expense. Your command may feel obligated to give you a number of opportunities to change your mind, so be firm and consistent. Your preferences may never be understood, but eventually they'll be accepted.

The timing of your ceremony may be difficult to arrange, especially if you're bringing guests from long distances, but it's best to arrange your turnover and leave so that your retirement ceremony is the last time you're at the command. The people who say "Goodbye!" to you on Friday may be a bit nonplussed to see you on Monday morning, and you may be perceived to have trouble letting go of the uniform.

☐ The Command's Farewell

Various groups at your command will want to say their goodbyes separately from your retirement ceremony. This usually involves a lunch or even a dinner party. Since they're doing all the work (and you're just showing up), it's hard to refuse. You'll have to work with the group leader to decide what's appropriate for you and for them.

If you're an extrovert who loves parties, then you'll enjoy yourself. However, it may also be scheduled during a particularly busy and stressful time along with your physical exams, your retirement checklist, and maybe even a move out of your home. Unless you're an extrovert, you may feel that the farewell gatherings are getting out of hand.

Keep talking with your friends and those group leaders. Make your desires simple and clear. If you feel that the affair is an additional burden on your retirement preparations, say so! One alternative would be to schedule it a week or two before your ceremony. Another alternative, especially if you're remaining in the area after retirement, would be to have it near the end of your terminal leave or even after you've retired. Have it at a local restaurant or park so that people won't be interrupted at the office. You'll have been away from the command for a while, so they'll want to see how retirement suits you. You'll have new stories to tell, and so will they. It's a great way to relax with the group without feeling the pressure to get things done.

Another common farewell issue is retirement gifts. Most retirees (and, frankly, their commands) would prefer a simple plaque or shadowbox. Others may want a more significant memento, or the command may have a custom of "awarding" a gag gift. Once again you'll have to make your desires known, especially to your friends who can take care of the details. For those who don't particularly care or who prefer to avoid the entire issue, you could ask that the command make a donation to a military charity of your choice. It's a simple yet noble gesture that will set the tone for your whole retirement.

☐ Saying "See You Later" to Everyone Else

Another surprise to many military retirees is the amount of time you'll spend saying goodbye. Between the retirement ceremony and the command's farewell you may feel that you've done enough: "It's taking too long, let's get this over with!" But a substantial portion of your day may be spent with people who drop by to chat for a few minutes, to figure out what you want for a part of a ceremony or a farewell, or even to ask a favor.

Be alert to these "chance" encounters. It's more than sharing a few war stories and setting up a tee time or a surf session. If you're a supervisor, you may be asked to write a number of recommendation or endorsement letters. This is your last chance to see that your troops get what they deserve. Like the retirement physical, it's much easier to do a good deed for someone while you're in the billet and wearing the rank. In a few weeks you'll be "just another retiree" whose thoughts may not carry any weight with an award committee or a selection board. When you present the situation to one of your perpetual fence-sitters who'd be great for a special program or a commission, you may be able to get them to commit to a decision in exchange for your recommendation.

A final note about your final day in the office: don't get ambushed. A prankster may have been planning something for months, or your chain of command may have "just one more thing." If you've been keeping up with your retirement checklist, you should be able to finish the last item well before your final day. On your absolute last day in the office you should show up on time and maybe even say a few goodbyes, but arrange to have an appointment or other reason to leave early – before lunch or even before 10 AM. Go to lunch but don't go back. Get your business done, finish your list, and go home!

5

Retirement for Reserves and National Guard*

W HILE CHAPTERS 2-4 described the "simplest" example of retiring early after at least 20 years of active duty, this chapter describes the more complicated considerations of retiring after a career in the Reserves or National Guard. Chapter 6 explains how to leverage your veteran's skills and experience to retire early with no pension at all! And if you're just starting out, Chapter 7 describes how to begin your journey to financial independence.

Another Way to Get to 20 Years for the Pension and TRICARE

Everyone who approaches the end of a military obligation has a tough decision: stay in or get out? The decision is even tougher after the first 10 years: stay in for retirement or get out while it's still easier to transition to a bridge career? Veterans aren't the only people grappling with that dilemma. Assignment officers are keenly aware that 15-year veterans are unlikely to leave before their 20th. As retirement gets closer, the choices get narrower and the nasty, difficult tours are more likely. At the beginning of a career it's bad enough to contemplate a hardship assignment just to reach the pension without realizing that your seniors are having even less fun.

When your head is down in the trenches, doing your best for the mission while preparing for promotions, it's hard to contemplate your alternatives. It's also scary to think about giving up a familiar career and a steady income. The uncertainty of starting over (and perhaps no paycheck for a few months) keeps many veterans on active duty for far longer than they may desire.

The following chapter has been written with the extensive input, review, and encouragement of "Deserat." She's balanced Reserve and civilian careers for decades and has served all over the world through multiple deployments. Best of all, she shared her knowledge in exchange for a surfing lesson. Thanks, Bridget!

"MICKEY-D" SAYS about his military career: I spent only about four years on active duty and another 20 in the Army Reserve. I stayed in the Reserve because I liked the folks in the units that I served in, and the extra pay was nice too. I never really considered retirement pay, much less TRICARE, at all. As I approached 20 years, I became very interested in the retirement check that would arrive at age 60. When I actually reached age 60, I soon realized that my TRICARE benefits were by far the best benefit of all. I have had a multitude of medical adventures since age 60, and the treatment that I have received at the Army medical center has been outstanding and cost-free.

It's very easy to serve a decade of active duty in blissful ignorance of the Reserves or National Guard. Some commands never even work with the Reserves or Guard, and there's little reason to teach active-duty personnel about those careers unless it's part of their mission. Each service's Reserve and National Guard units vary widely in duties, operating tempo, and policies. So for those who don't know the system, a very broad summary follows.

Members of the Reserves and National Guard can serve on active duty, drill status, or inactive status. (The details are more complicated than this overview.) Drilling is generally one weekend a month with two annual weeks of active duty, but there are many opportunities for longer periods of active duty. Some Reserve and Guard units may deploy every few years, requiring members to serve on active duty for 6-15 months. Other Reservists manage their individual careers and deploy every 5-6 years with or without their unit.

Every drill is worth a point of credit toward retirement, and every day of active duty is worth another point. Members have to earn a minimum annual number of points for a "good year" toward retirement. Retirement eligibility is reached after 20 good years (including any active-duty years), and the amount of the pension is determined by the number of points. Unlike an active-duty retirement, Reserve/NG pensions start payments at age 60. In general, Reservists and National Guard members will earn enough points during their career for a pension of about 15%-40% of an active-duty base pay scale. Some may earn more, and a few will earn quite a bit more. See the example at the end of the chapter, page 77, and Appendix C, page 155, for more details on calculating a Reserve/NG pension.

No one joins the military to get rich, and that's especially true of the Reserves/NG. Some Reserve components don't even pay for some forms of drilling or training and your pension doesn't start for years after you've retired. But you're not in it just for the money; you're improving your quality of life! The Reserves/NG can be a vast improvement over active duty because you'll have much more control over your assignments and better choices for work/life/family balance.

Active-duty members are at the constant beck and call of the assignment officer. Even after years of service they're still subject to hardship locations, unaccompanied duty, disrupted tours, and reassignment at "the needs of the service." If the assignment officer phones you, it's probably not good news.

In the Reserve/NG, though, you can decide how much time you want to devote to the military. You can do the minimum required number of drills and mobilizations. You can go on active duty for months at the same command. If other life events make it difficult to balance your military career, you can apply for inactive status, the military's version of unpaid leave. You can apply for schools and extra training or complete online work or correspondence courses for additional retirement points. You can complete a minimum assignment with a unit, "homestead" for years, or switch among different billets in the same geographic area. You can be your own best assignment officer with your career and your interests at heart.

Although the Reserve/NG pension doesn't begin until age 60, it's adjusted for both pay raises and inflation. When a member begins drawing retired pay, the base pay used for their first pension payment is taken from the latest pay charts. Even though a Reservist may have filed for retirement in 1990 at age 40 and spent 20 years awaiting the start of retired pay, in 2010 at age 60 they'll use the most recent pay scale in effect. Two decades of pay raises will hopefully have kept up with historic inflation, just as a pension with a cost-of-living-allowance increase will hopefully keep up with future inflation.

An even better benefit is that the pension is based on the pay chart's maximum longevity in that pay grade. A retiree may only have 20-25 years of service, but when the retirement payments begin, they may be paid at the longevity of 26-30 years of service in their retirement rank. The Department of Defense is willing to hand out these benefits in the hope that Reservists/NG will retire awaiting their pensions (and possibly be subject to wartime mobilization) instead of resigning.

As attractive as the pension may seem, there are additional privileges with very substantial financial benefits. Reservists/NG are eligible for low-cost health care while on active duty. Medicare doesn't start for most civilian retirees until age 65, but military Reserve/NG retirees are eligible for TRICARE at age 60 and TRICARE For Life after age 65. That's five extra years of military medical insurance for only a few dollars a month, and it makes a big difference in states where a private insurer's premiums can cost as much as $2,500/month. During the years when a Reservist/NG member is retired awaiting retirement pay, they're still eligible for access to the base and its commissary, exchange, fitness, and recreation facilities. They can still use benefits such as a VA loan and the GI bill. Some of these benefits may be subject to time limits or space availability, but they're a potent way to bridge the gap between a paycheck and a pension.

It's easy to transfer to the Reserves from active duty. (A short Reserve commitment might even be required after an active-duty obligation.) Active-duty service is credited toward the Reserve/NG retirement system. Veterans might even choose to live in the same area and drill at the same command, but the Reserve obligation is also a great chance to travel the world while working part-time. You can re-invent your life and your career, and you have far more control over your assignments.

Veterans can apply to rejoin the Reserves/NG months or even years later, and civilians can join without any prior military service.

Another advantage of leaving active duty for a Reserve/NG career is that it's a fresh start. When you're unhappy on active duty, it may be extraordinarily difficult to switch career tracks. You'll have to apply to your current career field's personnel managers to leave, and you'll have to apply to another career field's personnel managers to join theirs – where you're not always greeted with open arms and cries of joy. You'll be under the gun to learn a new system and to stay competitive for promotion. You might even be expected to start at the bottom of the new ladder, despite all your years of experience (and rank) in your former community. If for some reason you were actually passed over for promotion, it's next to impossible to recover from it and to remain competitive.

The Reserves/NG allows a do-over and maybe even a clean slate. It's a chance to not only change your lifestyle but your military specialty, your rating, your location, your duty station, and your environment. Instead of working hours of overtime for months to stay ahead of the pack, you can find a niche where you're more competitive. Reservists who don't get promoted will continue to be considered at subsequent selection boards and may even be permitted to remain in a drilling status, accumulating retirement credit even though they may not be paid for their drills.

SHE'D HAD IT with active duty. The first five years had been great, but marriage and two kids had given her a completely new set of priorities and put a strain on her work/life balance. Overseas duty used to be fun, but now it was a chore to adapt the kids to the culture and schools, and they just couldn't travel like before. She didn't feel that she could spend as much time at work or on duty as she used to. Unfortunately her commanding officer felt the same way and there was little chance that her latest performance evaluation would earn her a promotion. Leaving under these conditions was sad, but she felt there was no other choice.

Two years later her life had completely turned around. She was drilling in the Reserves and had even been promoted. Her husband was able to cover the family front during her drill weekends (good for him and the kids, as well as for her), and she was getting just enough work to feel fulfilled without being overwhelmed. Instead of trying to keep up, this time she felt that she was getting ahead and would even stay until retirement.

Extended Mobilizations

Deployments can be a drawback to balancing the Reserves/NG with a civilian career. For active-duty veterans, deployments are just another part of the lifestyle that includes extensive support and assistance for both the service members and their families. In the 20th century, Reserves/NG rarely deployed and family support (if any) was arranged by their unit instead of being a part of the active-duty system. In the post-9/11 era, however, the Reserves and National Guard have been heavily mobilized to support worldwide operations. It's now expected that the old system of "one weekend a month and two weeks a year" will also include "12-month deployments every five years."

Time (12-15 months) away from family and civilian career can be managed – or it can wreak havoc. Families may not be aware of the support offered by the military, or they may not understand the best way to tap into the resources. Civilian medical insurance may be disrupted by shifting to military health care. Employers are required by federal law to protect Reserve/NG pay and seniority, but a prolonged absence may still affect their working conditions and career opportunities. Skills can decline while projects move on without them and clients find other support. It's particularly difficult for those who are entrepreneurs in civilian life to keep their customers.

A relatively new benefit encourages Reserve/NG deployments by starting the pension earlier. Under current legislation, retirement pay would begin one day sooner for every day of deployment since January 2008. (Veteran's groups are lobbying to backdate this benefit to 9/11 or even earlier.) With a year or two of deployment for every decade of service, the result is that a Reserve/NG member could start their pension (and their health care benefits!) in their late 50s.

Avoid These Other Civilian-Military Pitfalls

You can balance a civilian career with a military commitment, but both sides have to make accommodations. Sometimes the arrangement is harmonious, especially if your career is in federal civil service or a military-support field. Other times you'll be tugged in different directions, particularly if you're a small business owner or a self-employed entrepreneur. Federal laws (and many states) protect your veteran's rights to employment and job status, but there are subtle variations of cooperation, compliance, and enforcement. When your upcoming National Guard deployment may affect your civilian career's opportunity to take on that special project, it's important to let your co-workers know. You don't want your occasional absence to cause a disruption and leave behind feelings of confusion or betrayal. If an adversarial relationship develops, you're sure to be on the losing side.

The most important aspect of balancing the two lifestyles is a detailed knowledge of your civilian-military leave policies. Your military chain of command will know what you rate, but your civilian boss will probably need your constant support and education. You may be able to take a leave of absence from your civilian job, or meet your military requirements on weekends and holidays. You may also be required to use vacation days to complete your Reserve duties. It's an awkward compromise and it's not always fair.

You and the Reserves/NG can also support your employer. Schedules and deployments are usually set months in advance, which can help you coordinate with your civilian staff. If your employer is particularly supportive of your Reserve commitments, put them in for an award! Advertise every win-win situation. Show off your military skills whenever they can be applied to your civilian job, and look for opportunities to use your civilian skills in your military leadership and management. Your experience in each world may help you get promoted in the other.

Family life is another challenge. If you're drilling, you'll miss a family weekend every month, perhaps with travel, and you'll be working at least two weeks a year in uniform – perhaps with more travel. National Guard units occasionally go on travel to train for weeks and then deploy for months. If you're raising young children or spending extra time with aging parents, you may have to transfer to inactive status for a few years until you can be flexible and mobile again. While you're deployed, spouses may have to deal with the military and health care bureaucracies on their own. It's important to make sure you both know how to find the information, assistance, and benefits that you've earned.

TIM REALIZED that his life could be better. He enjoyed military aviation, but he hadn't risen to the top of the pack, and he could see that his career wasn't going anywhere. He also felt that he was missing out on everything else – traveling the world, seeing other cultures, and hiking, climbing, and skiing. He didn't want to work long boring hours anymore, and he wanted more control over his time.

Five years later he had crafted a new life. The first year had been a little rocky and the money had been tight, but he'd finally worked

continued

out a system. Every winter he taught at a ski resort, although the pay was low and the cost of living was high. But the rest of the year was spent somewhere in the world on a six-month Reserve "hot fill" billet. They were happy to see him wherever he went. He had a talent for working on command center watch bills and explaining aviation issues to other services. The hours were long, but the pay was very good (frequently tax-free), and at the end of his orders he could spend a month or two exploring his new country. (He'd already seen Europe, the Middle East, and Southeast Asia.) After the next ski season he wanted to go to Eastern Europe and maybe travel in Russia.

Reserve/National Guard Retirement Eligibility

Retiring from the Reserves or National Guard is more flexible than from active duty. In the vast majority of cases, your retirement is based on at least 20 good years of service. You'll be tracking these years as you complete the minimum annual requirements, and when you reach 20 years your service will formally notify you via a letter of eligibility.

When you're eligible to retire, you may prefer to stay as long as you can. You may be successfully balancing the military with your civilian career and your family, and you might be able to continue your routine for years. The money may not be much, but it can greatly boost your tax-deferred savings. Military pay offers another stream of income to serve as insurance against civilian layoffs. Some Reservists/NG will even work in unpaid billets that only offer retirement points, in hopes of later qualifying for a paid billet or earning a promotion. As your children grow older you may be able to kick-start your military career with advanced schools, special programs, or extended active-duty mobilizations. In metropolitan areas with large military commands it's not unusual to serve with many Reserve/NG members in their late 40s or even mid-50s.

Retiring From the Reserves/National Guard

Reserve/NG retirement is even simpler than active duty. The letter of eligibility has already certified that the member is eligible to retire, and his/her retirement request sets the date. If a retiring Reservist/NG is actually on active duty (mobilized) at the time of retirement, separation procedures are executed just as for any demobilization. If a Reservist/NG is not on active duty, there is no DD-214, no medical/dental examination, and no other paperwork. They're transferred to "retired awaiting pay" status, issued a gray ID card, and waiting for age 60. At age 59½ another round of verification paperwork is completed, and the pension begins six months later.

The Department of Defense wants Reservists/NG to request retirement instead of resigning. One difference is that personnel "retired awaiting pay" could hypothetically be mobilized, although that has not happened in decades. (It would require a full mobilization for a congressionally approved war, not a presidential mobilization as was declared after 9/11.) Another difference is that requesting retirement keeps Reservists/NG on the pay seniority list. At age 60, the years of annual pay raises and longevity increases will be applied to your first pension check, which will be based on the current pay tables and the maximum longevity at that rank. A resigning Reservist/NG will not receive any of those increases, so the cost of avoiding any mobilization is being paid at the pay tables in effect at resignation – which by age 60 may be decades old and without any pay raises or longevity increases.

The Survivor Benefit Plan (SBP) is an important consideration for "retired awaiting pay" status. You may be waiting for the pension benefit for over two decades, and if you don't make it to age 60 you may want to ensure that some of this benefit is still available to your surviving loved ones. Retiring Reservists/NG can elect SBP coverage during the years between retiring and reaching age 60. No premiums are paid during this time. If you don't make it to age 60, your survivors receive their SBP payments. However, if you do make it to age 60, you will be required to pay two years of SBP premiums to recover the cost of your insurance during those years between retiring and reaching age 60. After paying two years of premiums the Reserve/NG retiree has the option to decline SBP or continue with it under the same rules as active-duty retirees.

Health Insurance While Retired Awaiting Pay

You do not have any military health care when you're retired awaiting pay. TRICARE will start at age 60 and Medicare/TRICARE For Life will start at age 65, but Reservists/NG awaiting a pension will need to buy other health insurance. Health care benefits may be one reason that some Reservists/NG continue to drill well into their 50s, although that should not be the only reason to continue to serve.

In late 2009 Congress authorized "TRICARE Retired Reserve," which began in fall 2010. The program is intended to offer a version of TRICARE Standard to retired Reservists and National Guard who are still under age 60. The program is not subsidized by the government and fees may be quite high compared to other TRICARE premiums. Premiums may even be higher than some civilian health care programs, but this program offers the first "gray area" coverage between retirement and age 60.

The Pension Starts at Age 60, But You Can Retire Right Now on Savings

One of the biggest advantages of the Reserve/NG is having an inflation-adjusted pension at age 60. It's paid by one of the world's most credible financial institutions. A civilian retiree, if they even have a pension, may not only have to wait years but also may have to worry that the company won't survive to pay the "guaranteed" pension. A military pension is even more highly rated than an insurance company's annuity, and you don't have to worry whether the insurance company will be able to make good on its future claim. The future is never certain, but a military pension is as close as you can get to a guaranteed stream of income at a known date.

The key to retirement as a Reservist/NG is planning your retirement finances around **multiple** streams of income. By the time you request retirement (awaiting pay), you'll have several different forms of savings. In addition to the pension at age 60, you'll also have your military Thrift Savings Plan account, as well as personal IRAs and taxable investments. If you're in the federal civil service, you'll have a second TSP account. If you're employed in the private sector, you'll probably have another tax-deferred savings account – a 401(k) – as well as other forms of deferred compensation. And if you're self-employed, there are several other ways to save through tax-deferred accounts.

Your challenge is to live off your savings until the tax-deferred accounts are available and until the Reserve/NG pension starts. The advantage of the pension is its known starting date, its inflation adjustment, and its high probability of payment. Your other savings may only have to bridge the gap between your retirement request and the start of your pension. You won't have to worry about outliving your money – only about making it last until the pension begins. In addition to spending down your taxable accounts, you can also tap your tax-deferred accounts if necessary, and, under some conditions, even without penalty. If your savings won't stretch to cover the whole gap between retiring and receiving a pension, then annual income can be augmented from part-time work or a civilian bridge career.

The planning and calculations may seem complicated or even overwhelming, but today's retirement-planning software is tremendously flexible at projecting multiple streams of income over an entire retirement. The next example and Appendix C on page 155 review the process. The Recommended Reading section has more information about different programs and their advantages on page 190.

Example Comparing an E-7 Active-duty Pension to an E-7 Reserve Pension

Consider 18-year-olds who enlist in the active-duty military, serve eight years while advancing to the E-6 pay grade, and then separate for a Reserve billet. Over the next 12 years as drilling Reservists they complete their "weekend a month, two weeks a year" drills while also mobilizing for two separate year-long deployments. By the eighth year in the Reserves they're also promoted to E-7, about the same point as their active-duty counterparts. Upon reaching 20 years of total service they request retirement awaiting pay.

When they joined the Reserves, their active-duty time was credited to their Reserve point count at the rate of one point for each day. The rules for drill points differ by service, but drilling "a weekend a month, two weeks a year" can conservatively be expected to average another 75 points each year over those 10 years. Each year-long mobilization would earn at least another 365 points.

continued

At retirement these Reservists would each have a total of at least (8 x 365) + (10 x 75) + (2 x 365) = 4,400 points. The current instruction specifies dividing by 360 (not 365) to convert points to equivalent years. So the percentage earned toward a Reserve pension would be 2.5% times the point count divided by 360, or 30.5%. An E-7 serving 20 years of active duty would base his/her pension on 2.5% x 20, or 50%.

The Reservists' inflation-adjusted pension doesn't start for another 22 years. (The inflation adjustment is set at the Consumer Price Index.) During those decades the military's E-7 base pay will rise by roughly the Employment Cost Index. The Employment Cost Index keeps pace roughly with inflation and the Consumer Price Index, so it's a reasonable approximation to assume that E-7 pay will rise at about the Consumer Price Index.

While awaiting retirement pay, Reservists will also be credited with the maximum longevity in that E-7 pay grade – 26 years – even though they only served 20 years. E-7>26 is a base pay of $4,521/month – nearly 15% over E-7>20. So in today's dollars (at the time of writing) that Final Pay pension would be 30.5% x $4,521/month = $1,381/month – or over $16,500/year. A High-Three pension would be based on three years of pay tables, or about 5% less than the Final Pay system.

The biggest difference between active-duty and Reserve pensions is that the active-duty E-7 would have served 20 years and started drawing their pension at age 38 at 50% of their base pay scale in effect at retirement. The Reserve E-7 would have started drawing their pension at age 60, using the maximum longevity and pay table in effect at that age. The extra 15% longevity would boost their pension to about 35% of the base pay of their active-duty counterpart (instead of 50%), and of course they'd be starting their pension 22 years later. However, their pension at age 60 is expected to have preserved its purchasing power at least as well as the pension that their active-duty counterpart has been drawing for over two decades.

When the 60-year-old Reservist finally starts drawing his/her pension, it will have a much higher dollar value (in future dollars) but should have roughly the same purchasing power as today's dollars. That income stream will continue to rise with its annual COLA. It will be one component of a retirement made up of tax-deferred accounts, taxable accounts, and any pensions from other (civilian or civil-service) careers. See Appendix C on page 155 for more details on balancing a Reserve pension with multiple streams of income.

6

Bridge Career Options

W HAT WILL YOU DO after your military service? Maybe your pension doesn't cover all of your expenses. Maybe you're not getting a military pension at all, let alone low-priced health care. Maybe you decided not to stick around for 20 years, or the Reserves/ NG didn't work out. At this point it can be hard to see the benefit of your military service, and you may even feel that you're no better off than a civilian! But keep reading. Lots of veterans have figured out how to retire early even without military benefits, and you can too. Indeed, this chapter includes two stories of vets who did that.

Retiring Without a Military Pension or Even the Reserves/National Guard

Financially, the best early retirement choice is staying on active duty until eligible to retire. But active duty is certainly not the easiest choice. When you're two years into that 20 with 18 to go, the "bolting" option seems much more likely. And if you feed a few frosty beverages to the typical military retiree, you'll eventually hear that the final two years were in many ways even harder than the first two. It's far easier to talk about making it to military retirement than it is to actually do it.

Just how hard could it be to stay for 20? If it's the surest and even simplest path to early retirement, then shouldn't everyone aspire to that goal? Yet after a few years in the ranks, you realize that there seem to be a lot more people separating from the military (even for the Reserves and National Guard) than retiring from it.

Statistics confirm that impression. If you're ready to get out of the military (and not even stay in the Reserves or National Guard), you have plenty of company. The vast majority of veterans don't even stay for 10 years. Only 15% of all veterans qualify for a pension (that includes Reserves/NG as well as active duty), and some services have an even lower retirement population.[1] The military's retention experts succeed by persuading only a minority of the recruits (both enlisted and officer ranks) to serve past their first obligation.

So, while resigning seems to be the most difficult path to a financially secure retirement, it's by far the most common one. Retention is much more highly correlated to career satisfaction and quality of life, although salary and bonuses can help. However, only you and your family can decide what's best for you, and at the end of the discussion you may find yourself saying, "Well, it's only money."

The first chapter of this book talked about the most powerful tools of a military retirement: low-cost health care and an inflation-adjusted pension. How in the world can a veteran achieve early retirement without either of these tools? It's not as easy, but it can be done. Civilians may not have these military options, but there are solutions. Nearly 20 percent of companies still pay fixed pensions, and some offer subsidized health care. Other retirees accumulate a larger investment portfolio (perhaps boosted by a lump-sum retirement account) and buy their own health care insurance until they're old enough for Medicare. A few retirees depend on the "multiple streams of income" approach described in Chapter 5, pages 76-77, and Appendix C, page 155. Still others bridge the gaps with part-time employment or extraordinary frugality.

The Safe Withdrawal Rate (SWR)

Regardless of their retirement benefits, **all** retirees have to manage their assets and their spending. The essential financial tool for assessing a retirement portfolio is the safe withdrawal rate (SWR): the rate at which withdrawals can be made without running out of money. The Recommended Reading section on page 184 lists many references and planning systems, but here's a brief summary of the four most popular financial options:

1. The 4% rule. The Trinity Study[2] was the first to show that a retiree's portfolio would almost always last for 30 years if retirees started their first year by spending no more than 4% of that portfolio, and then raising each subsequent year's withdrawals by the rate of inflation. Some principal is consumed nearly every year, and by the end of 30 years the portfolio may run out under extremely adverse conditions.

The Trinity paper spawned controversy and an entire industry of SWR analysis. What exactly is "almost always"? What about having enough assets to survive for 35 years, 40 years, or even 50 years of retirement? Is it really 4% or lower? Higher? How much can inflation change from one year to the next, and how bad can it get? What if we decide to consume less principal, or try to have some portfolio left after 30 years? If we have better data and more powerful analysis techniques, what else can we squeeze out of this?

Almost all retirees use 4% as a starting point or a spending tripwire. The Recommended Reading section lists many other references and approaches to determining your own SWR, from simple to extremely complex. While other retirees will spend the rest of their lives exploring all the subtleties of this approach, let's move on to the other three options.

2. **The dividend rule.** Many retirees take great comfort in only spending what their portfolios earn. Their portfolios use various combinations of dividend-paying stocks, high-quality bonds, rental real estate, and CDs instead of depending on growth equities or commodities. Each year's budget may be limited by last year's dividend income, or CDs might be spent during a recession while stock and bond dividends recover. To preserve the portfolio's purchasing power, dividends will have to rise at least as fast as inflation. The SWR is less than the portfolio's total dividend rate and almost always less than 4% per year. Spending may fluctuate with the economy or inflation, but the portfolio never runs out of money because principal is never consumed. However, the lower SWR requires a larger portfolio than the 4% rule, which usually means saving more or working longer.

3. **Multiple streams of income.** This option has almost as many variations as the 4% rule. Some retirees work part-time at their avocations (or develop new ones) for the rest of their lives. Others take great comfort in a more structured corporate environment with part-time employment, and the money certainly doesn't hurt. Some work a few mornings a week (or to qualify for health care benefits) as long as they're able. A few only work seasonally, to earn extra money for special spending occasions, or when their portfolio falls below a warning line. Rental real estate is a popular way to create a stream of reliable income with fewer working hours. Finally, many veterans combine a military pension with civil-service or civilian pensions and their savings to bridge the gap to Social Security.

4. **Frugality.** These retirees focus on expenses, not assets or income. They'll start with a bare-bones survival budget and add in various "luxuries" that depend on their portfolio's performance or their willingness to work for extra income. Before they'll go back to work, however, they'll happily devote a majority of their time to cutting waste or reducing expenses. They're more focused on the challenges of their lifestyle than its luxuries (or lack thereof). While very few frugal retirees may occasionally cross the line into outright deprivation, nearly every early retiree practices some aspect of this technique. It's also a very handy survival tool for a harsh economy, which we'll discuss more in the next chapter.

Early retirement finances will almost always be split among all four options. Many retirees still fondly recall the day in their working years when they updated their net worth spreadsheet and realized that they had enough to meet the 4% rule. Others have a lifestyle epiphany and begin aggressively cutting expenses, saving every spare penny, and carefully tracking their progress. A few save enough to pursue their avocation and happily take whatever payments come their way. A very few spend years or decades traveling the world's bargain countries or living a bare-bones lifestyle before settling down to a more traditional retirement in their dream location.

Ken's Early Retirement

HE'S BEEN active on early-retirement discussion boards for over a decade, but few know that he started his career in the military. He and his spouse raised a family and been happily retired for several years without any pension or benefits – just their savings. Today they enjoy their grandchildren and roam the country in their recreational vehicle, visiting with other early retirees whom they've met over the Internet.

Ken graduated from college and joined the Air Force just slightly ahead of the Vietnam draft. After flying various types of aircraft, he returned to Officer Training School as an instructor. In the late 1970s the Air Force was overcrowded with pilots, and retention was not a priority. The military budget was tight, pilots were competing for fewer aircraft with less flying, and the trend was clear. He had a great lifestyle in a warmer climate, a young family, and no desire to serve a hardship tour at a frozen northern base.

He was surprised to consider resigning because he'd long expected to retire from the military. He enjoyed flying and had been given several indications that he was on track for more promotions. The first few years weren't too bad, life was exciting, and he took great comfort knowing that a military pension and lifetime medical care would be waiting for him. But those plans had been made before he started a family. He'd already spent three of his eight years of service away from them, and they had a higher priority now. He left active duty at age 31 with an at-home spouse raising two young children, a small emergency cash fund, no retirement savings, and a mortgage.

The military can make it hard for veterans to appreciate how favorably their discipline, ethics, and skills compare to the civilian workforce. The military is a dangerous career, budgets are tight, and risk-taking may be discouraged. The chain of command can impose layers of bureaucracy in every direction and smother initiative. Military bearing and uniform appearance are under constant scrutiny. Supervisors and inspection teams relentlessly point out the slightest flaws in every aspect of duty. Performance assessments regularly give veterans the impression that they're barely capable of handling their current rank, let alone being promoted. It's no surprise that some can be made to feel as if they're worthless and weak, expecting to be ordered to drop and give 20.

Many veterans are surprised to discover how their military skills transfer to a civilian career. Employers are happy to hire workers who can just show up on time, let alone be ready to work safely and without drama. Ethics and honesty, always a military expectation, may seem much more flexible at a civilian workplace, and high standards can be a welcome surprise. Veterans are used to accomplishing miracles with few resources and are quite accustomed to being put on the spot by supervisors, co-workers, or customers. Workplace crises and even emergencies are no problem compared to a combat zone. Civilian budgets and supervision may still be tight, but veterans have long ago learned to work the system to reward initiative, stamina, and discipline.

KEN TOOK A 40% pay cut by leaving the military to become one of his new company's oldest "management trainees." Yet only six months later he was approached to help recruit other junior officers. His VP of Operations said he wanted to find more "like him" who could quickly grasp the technical and personnel issues of running a production floor. Most of the company's management hires had been recent college graduates who lacked the maturity and discipline needed to successfully lead a highly skilled group of older blue-collar workers. However in those days of "never trust anyone over the age of 30," the company had shied away from hiring anyone of Ken's age. His attitude and performance single-handedly changed their attitude. He later learned that his military background and the interpersonal skills he had shown during his interviews persuaded the executives to hire him as an experiment – one that succeeded far beyond their expectations.

Ken's company was one of the industry's best, but the industry itself was doomed to extinction by automation. The executives aggressively acquired other firms during years of consolidation and became a nationally known corporation with a significant market share – as well as significant profit-sharing contributions to the employee retirement fund. Although 401(k)s hadn't been created yet, he could deposit after-tax dollars in his retirement fund and the company contributed a share of its profits. He wanted to catch up on years of missed opportunities, so he quickly ramped up his contributions and maintained the pace for 27 years.

Ken didn't have any early-retiree role models back then, but he knew that he needed to take care of his family. As the industry's inevitable decline accelerated, he felt that his experience wouldn't easily transfer to yet another career. He needed a larger nest egg in the expectation of losing his job and having to take a significant pay cut in a new field. So, in his 40s, while his income was still rising, he and his spouse began aggressively saving for a bigger emergency fund, their children's college funds, and retirement. They eventually realized that not only could they fall back on their investments if he lost his job, but they might actually be able to retire early. His interest in early retirement blossomed as he discovered the Trinity study and the Internet's first early-retirement discussion groups.

Their portfolio grew along with their kids until they were off the "Mom and Dad, Inc" payroll, and then the savings really accelerated. In his early 50s and making great progress, Ken's comfort level grew as he learned more about portfolio survival, asset allocation, SWRs, and the early-retirement lifestyle. He and his wife decided to delay early retirement for an extra year to finish paying off their mortgage, and fully retired in their late 50s.

Ken's experience is all too familiar to most veterans and retirees. His military career prospects were bright, but starting a family completely reordered his priorities. Instead of continuing to sacrifice those priorities for another decade, or balancing family and civilian career with the Reserves or National Guard, he elected for a complete break. His family supported his choice and he was able to balance his new priorities with his new career.

Although he's not drawing a military pension, Ken used all of his military skills to create his new life. Not only does it take tremendous courage to make the leap from one career to another with minimal savings, it also takes planning, hard work, and self-confidence. His years of Air Force responsibility and accountability served him well.

Of the four approaches to retirement, the two that worked best for Ken were frugality and the 4% rule. Although their earlier frugality was imposed as much by necessity as by choice, he and his spouse continued the practice and quickly ramped up their savings. Eventually the portfolio reached a value that would support the 4% rule, but they delayed their retirement to pay off the mortgage for an extra margin of comfort. One reward for their years of sacrifice and savings was buying a recreational vehicle that's opened up a whole new lifestyle. Another reward is a growing tribe of grandchildren!

With a couple of nasty bear markets under his belt, Ken is certainly more concerned about the financial future of early retirement. He has a much greater appreciation for the value of dividends in minimizing the damage to a battered nest egg. But he says he wouldn't change his decision to retire early, and he's confident that their portfolio will continue to thrive.

Arif's Early Semi-Retirement

ARIF'S FIRST exposure to early retirement started as a platoon leader at Fort Hood. He noticed that his company commander was supporting his at-home spouse and family on just one salary. Arif's wife was about to be commissioned and he knew that they could do quite a bit with two Army incomes, especially when they turned into two Army pensions. Soon they bought their first duplex home, lived in one half, and rented out the other. They were collecting $1,500/month in housing allowances, but the rent was paying most of the mortgage. Suddenly they had plenty of cash flow to invest.

The TSP wasn't available to the military in those days, so their only other choices were IRAs and taxable accounts. They quickly discovered that they were much better at finding real estate investments than equities or bonds, so they put all their extra income into property. They bought two foreclosure bargains, hired a property manager, and kept on buying at their next duty station. As they gained more experience (and credibility with their bank), they continued buying foreclosed properties for 70 cents on the dollar. They managed some on their own and hired managers for the rest. By the end of their next tour of duty they owned 31 units in three states!

As Arif and his wife considered the choices for their next duty station, their rising rental income presented another option. They didn't have enough to live on without major spending cutbacks, but they knew they had the skills and experience to keep growing their largest stream of income. They had vacationed in Panama the year before and loved the country's culture, so they considered the challenge of relocating and managing their rentals from across the border. When they realized that their cost of living would be roughly half of their American budget, they submitted their resignations. They didn't have a Reserve obligation, and they didn't even have jobs!

Only a military veteran would contemplate this type of transition, let alone succeed at it. They built their real-estate experience on their own time, away from the Army, and they quickly learned what worked (made money) and what didn't. They could objectively critique their accomplishments and apply the lessons learned. Although the Army taught them how to lead and manage, they grew their own self-esteem and they didn't need the military to assess their property skills.

Other military advantages come from tackling big responsibilities at the beginning of a career. Very few people in their 20s are encouraged to lead dozens of experienced workers, care for large quantities of expensive and dangerous equipment, and execute a six-figure budget to train their people and accomplish a mission. Veterans have learned how to make tough decisions, develop a plan, and have the stamina to carry it out. It takes a tremendous amount of self-confidence to quit a career, move to a foreign country, and earn a self-employed living. Arif and his wife gained all of those strengths from their Army tours and their rental experiences.

ARIF AND HIS family quickly learned the concept of "Panama time." Their lifestyle became much less materialistic and more laid back. Their annual spending plummeted from $50,000 to $25,000, yet their quality of life dramatically improved. They had plenty of family time to spend with their young son, to improve their Spanish, to go to the gym every day, to take up scuba diving, to hire a house cleaner, and even to spend a few days at the local beach resort.

Two years later, self-employed with minimal health care insurance, they had everything they wanted. They worked on their own schedule, and their lifestyle could be called "early semi-retirement." They traveled to the U.S. several times a year to inspect their properties and as the American real estate market soared, they began selling them. Arif refers to it as "searching for 75-cent dollar bills." He even considered using the last of his GI Bill benefits for flying lessons.

When I showed a draft of this chapter to Arif, he had a personal update on the worst recession in decades:

"AS YOU KNOW, the real estate market has changed quite a bit. One of the biggest changes that affected us was the new federal lending rule that you can only have five mortgages. When that started we had about seven! We saw the Panama real estate market de-

continued

teriorating as well. Effectively these changes shut us out of the real estate business, so we went back to the drawing board and totally changed our lives again. We still have some rental units, but we also moved back to the U.S. last year and bought a pool service company. Despite being back to work, the lessons I learned from our two-year semi-retirement still guide me today. I've structured my work responsibilities to three days a week and I hire employees whenever the workload reaches five days a week. It's worked very well and keeps me focused on maintaining the freedom we enjoyed in Panama. We still keep our expenses low which allows us that flexibility. The moral of the story is to keep thinking outside the box and to take advantage of situations that life presents to you."

From platoon leaders to rental properties to small-business owners, Arif and his wife are still applying their military skills to attaining early retirement. Now that they've had a taste of early retirement, they've balanced their work with their lifestyle and they know what to do to enjoy it full-time. Not only do they have the skills and discipline to get there, but they've chosen one of the most successful methods – owning their own business.[3]

Ken and Arif represent both ends of the bell curve of military-transition experiences, and in two different centuries, but they share many common aspects. Both started their military careers intending to go all the way to a pension, but both became progressively disillusioned with the military and more focused on their families. Unlike many civilians, both of them were forced into a transition decision by an impending transfer. They used the final months of their service to make their plans and then executed them. Once they'd made the transition they continued to control their expenses, save as much as they could, and grow their wealth.

Ken's retirement is still based on the 4% rule, although he appreciates the value of dividends during a recession. Arif may use those systems some-day, but for now he's living on multiple streams of income and a frugal lifestyle. If both continue to grow their portfolios, then they could attempt to live only on dividend income, but both have already won the game. Neither has any need to try to run up the score by taking on more risk to pursue greater wealth. Instead, they can continue to enjoy their lives amid the security of knowing that they have enough.

These examples can help you tailor your own transition to your preferences and circumstances. Finishing 20 years of active duty may seem like the simplest financial option for a COLA pension and low-cost health care, but lifestyle and priorities may dictate otherwise. The Reserves and National Guard offer a wide variety of options for work-life balance, but success depends on having complementary military and civilian careers that allow switching between the two for mobilizations or for lengthy, complicated projects. Completely quitting the military is another option. It offers transition benefits and the GI Bill to build on years of training and practical experience that is valued by all employers.

There are many paths to retirement. They involve different career choices, different investment assets, different budgets and lifestyles, and even different withdrawal methods during retirement. You will find your own path. And when you do, you can share your wisdom with the future retirees who are reading the next chapter.

7

Move in the Right Direction

THIS CHAPTER PRESENTS your journey to financial independence so that you're ready when you reach your own retirement decision point. Whether you're beginning your career or if you've just made early retirement a new goal, this chapter gets you started. The chapter concludes with an essay on why the "fog of work" gets in the way of long-term planning.

Military Compensation and the Lifestyle

One of the more prolific posters on www.Early-Retirement.org, SamClem, has a very insightful comment on the military's care and feeding of its members:

> *"The military has a highly paternalistic compensation and social structure. The medical needs of you and your family are tended to. Have another kid? We'll give you a bigger house. Having trouble paying your bills? Your boss will see that you get counseling. Getting fat? The system will 'help' you get thinner. The collective will see to your needs in exchange for your loyalty and service."*

The military will tell you about preparing for retirement, and you'll be offered ways to save for financial independence, but you'll have to do your own retirement planning. You'll have to apply the resources in ways that the Department of Defense never imagined. The decisions you make in your 20s and even 30s will have a large impact on your financial independence in your 40s.

However, finances may not always be your top priority. Life decisions like education, marriage, and family involve far more important considerations than "just" money. Of course, if your decisions happen to give you a head start on financial independence, time and compound interest will take care of the rest. So, although the military may happily subsidize your lifestyle with a bigger base house, savings-plan deductions, or other benefits, you'll need to take the reins and do your own planning. It might be better in the long run to save additional funds in taxable accounts, or to build equity by owning an off-base home, or even to invest in rental property. Your basic military skills (and the transition assistance programs) will help you start a bridge career, but you'll have to use your own initiative and planning to achieve retirement.

Many decisions will be made for you during your military career – duty stations, training, deployments, and how to handle combat. You'll also be making your own life decisions: a college degree, finding a partner, buying a house, starting a family, and leaving the military for a bridge career or early retirement. If you consistently make your military career the most important aspect of your life, then those life decisions may be made for you by the military.

That's not a bad thing, especially if you're a great leader who makes the military your avocation, but SamClem's "collective" may not always reward your devotion in the manner you'd intended. The vast majority of veterans enjoy the military as a profession for only a few years, and only a few stay for 20 years. The work-life balance is a perpetual struggle, and it's important not to be so focused on work that you miss the life opportunities around you. If the military is not your avocation and you'd rather make your own life decisions, then you'll need to stay alert for opportunities that will lead you to financial independence. Later in this chapter, we'll talk more about dealing with the "fog of work," which can get in the way of long-term planning, but the first step is to start saving.

Start Saving Early

There's not enough space here to discuss all the subtle nuances of budgeting, saving, and investing. Thousands of other books handle the details of how to save for different situations, what types of investments you should allocate your money to, and how your portfolio should change with age and life situation. The best of those resources are listed in the bibliography on page 177 and frequently discussed on websites like www.Early-Retirement.org. This book is only going to present the principles and show you how to get started.

All the financial retirement books, websites, and TV shows boil down to one piece of advice: **save money**. The size of your retirement portfolio depends on the amount of money you've put into it and the length of time that it can grow. If you save more money, you won't need as much time. But most of us will never have an opportunity to save hundreds of thousands of dollars a year, so the most important factor becomes time. The only way to maximize that time is to start saving **now**. Even $50 per paycheck starts a habit that will grow for the rest of your career.

The race to retirement is a marathon, not a sprint, so it's no problem to start at a slower pace. Most military retirees will grow their portfolios for a minimum of 20 years. The first year or two of paychecks may only support a small amount of savings. Once the saving habit is formed, however, it's easier to keep up with it through every pay raise and promotion.

The "savings mindset" is far more important than a dollar amount or the percentage of a paycheck. The key is to spend money only on the things that add value and joy to **your** life and to save for the goals that will add even more value. Spending a dollar today may bring value, for a few happy moments or for many months of pleasurable use, but that dollar invested at 4% for 20 years will more than double in worth. The spending question is not "Can I afford it?" The **saving** questions are "Which do I value more? Do I want to enjoy this today, or do I want to save the money for retirement?" Another way to evaluate spending is in terms of work: "Do I want to work xx hours/days/weeks to pay for this, or would I rather save the money for retirement?"

Focus on the financial decisions that have a big impact on the budget. Jeff Yeager, the author billed as "The Ultimate Cheapskate," claims that saving money doesn't start with a $3 cup of coffee. Many financial authors and websites show how the "latté factor" adds up when a small daily expense is invested and compounded for 20 years. However, this is such a small expense that you're unlikely to deliberately avoid spending it and even less likely to put it into savings. You'll probably end up spending it somewhere else, or you'll spend your whole day discovering $3 temptations. Even worse, every day you're denying yourself a small pleasure that you're not putting to work for you somewhere else – so why suffer needlessly?

Instead of agonizing over small daily expenses, consider your fundamental lifestyle choices that will have an immediate and large impact on your savings. Start with your housing costs. Do you want to rent or own a luxury condo or McMansion in the expensive part of town, or would a more modest home closer to work serve your needs better? If you're going to spend most of the next year in the desert or at sea, do you really need a costly place to store your stuff? If you're living closer to work, could you spend less time commuting and maybe even bicycle or walk? If you're not spending a lot of time commuting, then do you really need a hot sports car or a haul-anything truck? Can you buy a cheaper (used?) vehicle and drive it into the ground? These decisions will save you hundreds of dollars a week, far more significant than the $3 cup of coffee.

While you're considering what's important in your life, see if your spending matches your values. The only way to understand your progress toward retirement is to track your spending. You want to save money, invest it, track the progress of those investments, and reach a portfolio size that supports your lifetime spending. The only way to calculate how much you'll need to reach your goal is to know how much you're spending. The only way to build a budget and to understand your expenses is to track your spending.

Tracking your spending is critical, but the **way** that you track it is up to you. Retirees use just about any method – expensive budgeting/accounting programs, free software, spreadsheets, handwritten notebooks, or even cash in envelopes for different spending categories. You have to develop a habit that works for **you** – saving receipts during the day and entering them onto a computer that night, entering purchases in a notebook as you go about your daily routine, or simply spending until that envelope runs out of money and then waiting until it's refilled by the next paycheck.

Frugal Living is not Deprivation

The military teaches everyone how to live an extraordinarily frugal lifestyle. No matter what reputation your service has, at some point you've lived in a very small room with a narrow bed and little storage. Maybe you did without a room or even a bathroom for quite a while, let alone a bed, and all your possessions had to be carried on your back in one piece of "luggage." Food was mass-produced or delivered in a box, snacks were hard to come by, and maybe you missed an occasional meal. Entertainment was rudimentary at best – no high-definition satellite TV or Internet access, let alone clubbing downtown!

If we all know how to live as cheaply as Tibetan monks, then why don't we practice that lifestyle and save 80% of our paychecks? We'd all set new records for early retirement! Veterans could eat all of their meals in the galley, spend their spare time reading library books or studying for advancement exams, and work out in the (free) gym. No money would be wasted on gasoline, let alone energy drinks, alcohol, tobacco, or video games. No one would even need to buy civilian clothes.

The irony of this example is that we all actually do know people who live like that. They're always saving their money, rarely socializing, and hardly ever going out. The problem with this single-minded focus on a spartan lifestyle (and its extremely high savings rates) is that it's very difficult to sustain. Life is boring, unfulfilling, and frustrating. These people seem to be pretty one-dimensional and very little fun to be with. Maybe they have a very good reason for squeezing the most out of every nickel, or maybe they can't help themselves, but it doesn't look like a way to enjoy a career or a life. They'll meet their short-term goals, but in the long term they'll drive themselves (and everyone around them) nuts.

Frugality is just simple living – a lifestyle that avoids waste. Extraordinary frugality, however, can be deprivation. Everyone understands how to avoid waste, but everyone also has a standard of living they're not willing to give up to achieve that level of avoiding waste. Early retirement benefits from frugality, but it does not require extreme frugality.

The difference between frugality and deprivation is personal and derived from your values. Everyone has a line between the two that they choose not to cross. The difference is that frugality feels good and makes you enthusiastic about reaching your goals. It's a challenge, and when you're doing well, you feel like a winner. You might not even miss the materialistic lifestyle that you're doing without. Deprivation is always doing without for a higher priority, willingly or not. Frugality matches your values and usually frees up quite a bit of savings that can be applied toward financial independence. You're living a life that you enjoy and you're making progress toward your goals – it's easy to feel good about it. Deprivation, however, rarely matches your values and feels more like slavery than volunteering. You may be making great progress, but it's definitely not easy and you will not feel good about it. Prolonged deprivation is extremely difficult to voluntarily sustain and usually leads to unhappiness.

The military teaches frugality (while imposing deprivation), but society does not always value frugality. We even have expectations of the ranks:

junior officers are seen driving hot cars, senior enlisted have hefty pickup trucks or SUVs, senior officers buy luxury vehicles and nice houses with lots of creature comforts and big yards; even junior enlisted may stand out among their barracks peers with a nicer laptop or a complex cell phone. If you're one of the few who can't flash an attention-getting possession, then you may be pitied. And everyone teases the junior officer driving a 10-year-old hatchback – or riding a bicycle!

Frugality may occasionally put you at odds with the standards of a materialistic society. The more frugal you are, the more you may appear to be "left out." Again the difference between frugality and deprivation is how you feel about it. If you relish the challenge, enjoy the achievements, and have fun while saving money, then you're doing great. If you're amused by the comments of your shipmates, then your frugality reflects your values (and probably your net worth). If you're feeling "left out" or even unhappy about the lifestyle remarks, however, you've probably crossed the line into deprivation. You need a critical short-term goal to endure deprivation for long, or you need to modify your values.

An interesting aspect of frugality and deprivation is that they can change your values, maybe even permanently. An extreme example of this is the Great Depression. In the 1920s a significant part of society was living very materialistic, even luxurious lives. In the 1930s many suddenly found themselves struggling to find enough food and stay warm, let alone have a job or even luxuries. They didn't volunteer for deprivation, but they quickly became extraordinarily frugal and managed to cope with the trauma. Over the years the habits became ingrained and part of their value system. When the Depression and World War II rationing ended, these members of The Greatest Generation didn't completely revert to their carefree spendthrift ways. We all know people of that era who can whip up a gourmet meal out of leftover cornflakes. They can fix anything in the home and think nothing of (gasp) walking to their destination. They even know how to do without! The other side of their frugality, though, is that many of these people will not spend money. They may still shun mortgages or credit cards, refuse to invest in the stock market, and won't buy newer technology or update their skills. They may castigate others for waste and may even have difficulty treating themselves to a luxury without feeling guilty. Their values were significantly changed by the earlier trauma, and they may struggle with what they see as modern society's degenerate lifestyle.

Many people see frugality as tedious, time-consuming labor. Once again, it depends on what you value. Cooking a meal from scratch is almost always more effort than dining out or picking up fast food. But you may feel that you get more value from preparing your own healthy, creative, high-quality meals. You might enjoy cooking as a hobby, not endure it as a chore. You may think that restaurant meals lack your talent for nutritious ingredients, proper seasoning, and creative presentation. The crowds, waiting, noise, and traffic might be discouraging. Or perhaps you prefer to save dining out for special occasions, and the experience would be less enjoyable if you did it every day. But while you're quite happy to eat at home and save your money instead of dining out, you may draw the line at rinsing and re-using plastic bags. It doesn't matter to you that others see this labor as keeping waste out of landfills. You're not willing to spend your time on the same goal.

Frugal zealots may be accused of taking advantage of others. For example, there's nothing wrong with choosing to drink water during a restaurant meal (instead of sharing a pitcher of another beverage) or to order smaller, cheaper menu items. However, if you're sharing with others, it's wrong to skip your turn to buy the next round of drinks, to help yourself to food that you're not paying for, or to skimp on your portion of the tip. That's not being frugal – that's being cheap. Frugality means avoiding waste and spending money on the things you value, not tricking others into spending their money on you.

Practicing frugality is not an all-or-nothing lifestyle. Learn as many techniques as you can and then choose the ones that you feel bring value to your routine. You may enjoy the daily challenge or you might decide to only be extra frugal if you had an emergency expense that month. You may adopt just one or two ideas (like bicycling for short trips) and then expand them (commuting or taking a bicycle trek for your next vacation). Drying one or two loads of laundry on a clothesline may be no problem when you're single, but the labor might be a bit much when you're raising a family of young children who can't yet do their own laundry. Monitor your spending, decide what's worth your effort, and change your habits as necessary.

Families can adopt frugality very easily and raise children with strong life skills. If you attempt to impose deprivation on your family, however, you'll be facing rebellion in the ranks. People will have to either choose to upgrade their lifestyle or change their values until deprivation eases up to frugality. If you're imposing deprivation on them, you may not get the cooperation you expect. Be patient and be ready to compromise.

Payroll Deductions

Parents and financial advisers use dozens of sound-bite homilies to get your money into an investment account before you're subjected to temptation. "Pay yourself first." "Out of sight, out of mind." "You can't spend it if you don't have it."

As annoying as that advice may be, it works. Frugality and budgeting help you align your spending with your values. If saving isn't a top priority, it will never be an important part of your budget, and you won't save enough to let compounding work its retirement magic.

Instead of having to compare every daily spending decision against your savings goals, though, you can set a savings goal and then put it on autopilot. After you build your budget and decide how much you can afford to save, use your payroll deductions and allotments to make it happen automatically. Try to maximize your contributions to the Thrift Savings Plan. Then consider an allotment to a fund company for your IRA. When the remainder of your paycheck arrives in your checking account, have an automatic deduction send some of it to a taxable investment account. Sweep more of it to a savings account and leave only that month's budget in your checking account. Whatever savings and investing goals you choose, let technology take care of it for you every payday so that you're not tempted to "adjust" the priorities every month for a little lifestyle upgrade. When deductions whisk the money away before it's in your hot little hands, it's easier to conserve what's left and make it last until the next payday. You won't be tempted to rationalize yet another month of spending while feeling that you just can't seem to save as much as you hoped.

A huge opportunity comes with every annual pay raise, longevity pay raise, special pay, bonus, and promotion. These are the windfalls that you may be able to learn to live without and can send straight to savings. Some pay raises are more permanent (annual raises, promotions) than others (combat pay, hazardous duty pay, bonuses). Inflation will also continue to eat away at a budget, and a growing family will always grow more expensive. But instead of increasing your spending in anticipation of more pay, try to raise your savings rate. A good compromise between frugality and deprivation would be to attempt to save at least 80% of every extra pay. If you try that for a couple of months and it's causing too much pain, you can reduce the savings percentage. It's far less painful to ease up on the savings rate than to try to increase it!

SAMCLEM AND his spouse saved their early-retirement nest egg the way most people should – plain, boring monthly contributions to their savings and investment accounts. They never missed the money, nor were tempted to spend it, because they never saw it. They started with $250/month after commissioning and raised it every year. With every promotion or longevity pay raise, they added a significant percentage to their monthly contribution to savings. By the time he retired they were saving $1,400/month.

The Thrift Savings Plan, IRAs, and Taxable Investment Accounts

Now that you have money to save, where should you put it? There are two basic concepts that should guide all of your investment decisions: minimization of taxes and minimization of expenses. There are hundreds of different investing techniques and asset classes, and thousands of different types of investments, but study after study has shown that these are the two most critical aspects for the vast majority of investors. With these two fundamentals, other advanced techniques may improve portfolio returns. However, without them, almost nothing else can overcome the drag of taxes and expenses.

If you can invest money before you have to pay taxes on it, then you can put more money into your investments. The less you have to pay in fees, the more money you have compounding for you. And the longer you can avoid paying taxes on an investment's profits, the more you have and the longer that money can compound. You'll attempt to exploit each of these concepts to the limits of the law for as long as you can.

One military benefit applies all three concepts simultaneously: the federal Thrift Savings Plan (for both federal civil-service employees and the military). This is a tax-deferred account combining the world's largest index funds with the world's lowest expenses. Your payroll contributions come from before-tax money (up to the legal limit) and you don't have to pay taxes on TSP funds until you withdraw them. Better still; the fund's expenses have been dropping as their assets have been growing. After starting the 21st century with expenses of three basis points (0.03%), the TSP expense ratio was as low as 1.9 basis points in 2007.[1] Even Vanguard Investment's expense ratios are higher than that of the TSP.

The TSP is your ultimate savings autopilot. After you sign up, you set your contribution level on your service's payroll website. You can send over 90% of your pre-tax pay to the TSP as you want, and you may be able to contribute special pay and bonuses as well. You can change it every month. When you meet the annual limits, the TSP will stop deducting contributions from your pay for the rest of that year.

The TSP is probably the preferred retirement savings system for the vast majority of veterans because of its pre-tax pay contributions, its tax deferral, and its low expenses. But once its contributions limits are reached, what next? If you can save more money, then you can put it in an Individual Retirement Arrangement (IRA).

There are two types of IRAs: conventional and Roth (named for the sponsor of the enabling legislation). Each type of IRA has its own advantages and disadvantages, and you may be able to contribute to either or both (while remaining within the overall contribution limit). IRAs are similar to the TSP because both will grow tax-deferred and have very specific withdrawal rules. The difference is that you have to select your own IRA account custodian (financial company) and can choose from a much wider range of assets and funds. The main advantage of an IRA is that it's another tax-deferred method of investing for retirement. IRAs have lower contribution limits and higher expenses than the TSP so they're usually a second choice to that program, but you have more control over how the account is handled and more choices over its investments. The TSP will even implement a Roth 401(k) provision to enable servicemembers to contribute after-tax pay to their TSP account.

When you're in your 20s and 30s, focus on contributing to the accounts. Let them compound and grow for at least 20 years. Don't worry about future withdrawals. There will be plenty of time to design a withdrawal plan when you're ready to retire, and there may be plenty of changes to the withdrawal rules before then. Both the TSP and IRAs have several methods of withdrawing the funds. They're designed to take monthly contributions from an early age, compound them for decades, and disburse them for many years after retirement. In most cases, early withdrawals incur a heavy penalty (and taxes) if they're taken before you're eligible. However there are penalty-free methods of borrowing or withdrawing some of the money before the minimum age of eligibility. Your TSP/IRA goal is to build them without being tempted to tap into them before you're retired. You can get your money back if you really need to (usually at a penalty), but the system is designed to keep you from acting impulsively. The withdrawal systems are far beyond the scope of this book but the Recommended Reading section has several references that will turn you into a TSP/IRA expert. For now, remember that your retirement planning will include other assets that you'll spend first in retirement while you're letting your tax-deferred accounts compound as long as possible.

What are these other assets? Is it possible to save more than your TSP and IRA limits? Sure, and the more you save early in your career, the sooner you'll be able to retire.

The TSP and IRAs are the only tax-deferred savings plans available to the vast majority of veterans. At any time, however, more money can be saved in taxable accounts. They're referred to as taxable accounts because you pay annual taxes on the profits and whenever you sell an asset. Although profits are taxable, the goal is still to maximize savings while minimizing expenses and taxes.

Taxable accounts are as simple as opening a checking/savings account with a bank or a credit union, and as complicated as a financial brokerage account. The simpler your plan, the easier it is to execute. The vast majority of veterans will open an account with a mutual-fund company, such as Fidelity Investments or Vanguard, to buy low-cost index funds. On pages 106-108 we'll talk about what types of assets and funds to consider, but for now your focus should be on saving as much as possible for as long as possible.

After setting up TSP and IRA contributions, a veteran's next priority should be funds for emergencies and short-term goals. An **emergency** is a car repair, fixing a home's broken water pipe, or a short-notice round-trip plane ticket to help a loved one. Emergencies are not material items like a new truck, an outfit for a business/social event, or concert tickets; those are short-term goals. A **short-term** goal is a savings program for anything that meets your values and could happen in the next few years. It could also include a house down payment, college tuition, a wedding, or even a fantasy vacation. Your budget includes short-term savings goals for entertainment as well as lifestyle upgrades.

The emergency and short-term funds should earn more interest than a checking account, but there should be zero risk of loss. The two most popular types of accounts for this money are money-market funds or certificates of deposit (CDs). The best rates for these two accounts are usually found at credit unions and banks. The size of the fund is up to you and your goals – anywhere from one to eight months' pay for an emergency fund. The fund may need to be bigger if you're transferring to a new duty station or leaving the military, but as long as you expect a biweekly paycheck you can minimize the size of your emergency fund.

If you've studied investment returns, you know that you pay a price for financial security. Your money-market funds and CDs are almost always insured against loss, but you receive a much lower rate of return than you would in high-yield bonds, technology stocks, or other investments that have a risk of loss. It can really hurt to park your money in a 3% CD when everything else in the world seems to be paying 6%, and it's tempting to chase a higher yield.

Don't do it. You're saving this money for emergencies and for important short-term goals. This is not the account to be used for maximizing returns by risking short-term losses – that's for the TSP, IRAs, and long-term taxable accounts. A short-term account does earn a lower return, but its payoff comes when you need the money. It's much easier to sleep at night if you know that you have the money available to cover an emergency without having to use a credit card or even get a payday loan. And although a CD may only pay 3% for years, the real savings come from the discounts given to those who can pay cash. You want to be the buyer who can swoop in on a bargain with money in hand, not the desperate seller who needs the money to pay for an emergency. Your cash makes Craigslist sellers and contractors very happy to give discounts, and that's the ultimate payoff for short-term savings.

Once you've planned your savings for emergencies and short-term goals, the final taxable account in every veteran's portfolio is for long-term investments. These funds will be needed for far-off goals of at least five years (such as a house down payment) and possibly even longer (kid's college tuition, retirement). Although they're not tax-deferred like the TSP or an IRA, these investments can be placed in similar assets like equity index funds. Taxes and expenses can still be minimized by using funds that don't trade frequently (low turnover) and that don't distribute a lot of dividends or capital gains. Most of them grow their share price or issue only qualified dividends which are taxed at lower rates.

Real Estate: Renting Versus Buying

Everyone in the service knows a military real-estate mogul. They're shipmates or other veterans who always seem to be looking at real estate, working on their home, and maybe even renting out a house as a landlord or investing in commercial property. They may not care about the cars they drive or the best restaurants, but their eyes light up when they start talking about home improvement or mortgages. They can tell you the best parts of town for finding a great quality of life, how to buy a good cheap "sweat equity" house, and where to look for property-management opportunities. They can even tell you what parts of the country they want to be stationed in to find good real estate, not just a good life. Real estate is more than a hobby to them – it's almost a side business and maybe their true avocation.

As you talk with these self-professed enthusiasts, you'll learn that they're handling assets worth hundreds of thousands of dollars, maybe five or even ten times their annual pay. They're doing it with **leverage**. Very few veterans actually own their homes debt-free because it takes years of saving to buy a home outright, and most veterans will move at least a half-dozen times during a 20-year career. Instead they're buying homes with a fraction of their own money, perhaps only 5%-20%, and borrowing the rest. They're paying their mortgage from their salary, housing allowance, or a tenant's rent and hoping that when it's time to sell, the value of the home has appreciated enough to give them a profit. If the real estate market is doing well, then their leverage bet pays off handsomely. It might even fund their retirement! If the real estate market is doing badly, though, then they'll lose money. You'll almost never hear people talk about their real-estate failures, either, so their "silent losses" make investing in property seem like a guaranteed road to financial success.

Most veterans confront the same decision with every transfer to a new duty station: live on base, rent, or buy a home? Each decision has its own merits, and they're not always financial. At some billets or overseas duty stations you may be required to live on base, while U.S. locations may have waiting lists of months or even years for base housing. You may prefer to live on base (especially if you're "on call"), or you may want to live out in the civilian community or near better schools for your kids. If you expect to be at a duty station for a number of years, you may be tempted to buy your own place.

Even worse, SamClem's "military collective" might influence your decision with a housing allowance. It's never been a better time to live off-base. Two decades ago the military's housing allowances barely covered a home payment, let alone utilities and insurance, but today's allowances cover nearly all of the average homeowner's expenses. As you're promoted, your housing allowance rises even if you're still living in the same place! Given the opportunity, it seems almost criminally wasteful not to put the government's free (and untaxed) housing allowance to work for you.

Before you grab the money and run to town, though, consider how this spending matches your lifestyle and your values.

- Is the base housing better or worse than the community?
- Will you have a better commute, perhaps even bicycling or walking to work, or will you be spending an hour a day sitting in traffic?
- How much time will you be spending in your house, especially if you're deploying soon?
- Where will your kids have better schools?
- Living out in town may put you among locals and "real" life, but it may also deprive your family of the special sense of community found among military families living together with shared sacrifices.
- If you're deployed for months, it may also deprive them of easy access to repair help and contractors.
- Are you a "house person" willing to tackle your own projects?
- Would you rather let a landlord take care of the home you're renting?
- Do you want to be responsible for your own maintenance and repairs, or would you rather let contractors fix your base home while you spend your time doing things that you value more?

Once you've settled on your values and lifestyle, the challenge becomes using your housing allowance as effectively as possible. You're not required to spend every penny of it. You might be able to find a place that costs only 90% of the allowance, or even 75%. Maybe it makes more sense to buy a duplex and rent out half of it while living in the other side, effectively gaining two sources of income (your allowance and the rent payments from your tenants). Consider all of the costs of housing, not just the rent or the mortgage payment. "Other" expenses include deposits, down payments, mortgage insurance, financing fees, closing costs, utilities, community association fees, escrow accounts, homeowner's or renter's insurance, property taxes, and commuting. These miscellaneous expenses might not seem like much, but they quickly add up to a significant impact when you've been paying those bills for a year or two. There are some tax advantages to owning a home, but the expenses can be far more costly.

While real estate (and its leverage) may seem to be the perfect path to military riches and retirement, you might not be able to afford the risk of a loss. Every recession shows millions of unfortunate homeowners that real estate prices can go down as much as they go up, and financial leverage is not a good idea if you're unemployed or can't find a rent-paying tenant. Home builders and mortgage banks love to sell to veterans because they tend to have steady paychecks and subsidized home-buyer's programs. However, you're also at risk of moving every few years, and buying/selling a home is a high-cost transaction that can quickly consume any profits. Being a landlord from another time zone (maybe even another country) is begging for trouble, and you may not have enough rent to be able to afford a full-time property manager. Adjustable mortgages, chronic rental vacancies, or selling a home that's lost its value will wreck a veteran's investment portfolio faster than almost any other financial decision.

ONE MILITARY officer couple, each with their own housing allowance, felt compelled to own their home. It was just too much money to let it go to waste! Their first condo (in a busy East Coast military town) had high buying and selling costs, and they lost a few thousand dollars during the three years they owned it. Their second condo (in California) skyrocketed in value, and when they sold three years later they earned over $30,000 on their $15,000 down payment.

Flush with success, they put every penny of their profits (and quite a bit more of their savings) into their Hawaii home. Deciding to live in paradise forever, they chose to pay off the home as quickly as possible with a 15-year mortgage at a slightly better interest rate. The higher payments used nearly every penny of their allowances, but they were confident that they'd succeed.

The economy and the assignment officers deemed otherwise. As Hawaii's housing market imploded and their home lost 40% of its value, they were unexpectedly ordered back to California. They decided to rent out the house rather than attempt a short sale or risk a foreclosure, but they lost hundreds of dollars a month for over three years. The additional expense of tenant turnover (and the home's unexpected repairs) added to their financial burden and their stress. They survived the ordeal, but they lived a very frugal lifestyle for several years to keep their ownership in a depreciating asset that, over 20 years, has only gained in value at about the rate of inflation.

Moving off-base is not a simple decision. Even if it seems to be the right choice for you and your family, renting or owning is another complex lifestyle/financial decision. Once you've decided those questions, you still have to ensure your housing costs are within your means and that you're saving the excess. Finally, consider whether you want to add to all your other lifestyle burdens by tackling the responsibility and risk of being a landlord. While it sounds like a no-brainer to buy that duplex and rent out the other side, the actual process is more complex and financially treacherous than it may appear.

If you're reasonably confident you'll be spending the majority of your career at that location, or at least willing to be a long-term landlord even while you're stationed somewhere else, then you'll likely earn a profit. However, depending on local conditions and the economy, you might have more lucrative places to invest your money – and there are certainly easier ways to invest it. If you're buying real estate just because it seems like the quickest way to get rich, you may also learn that leverage is a slippery path to foreclosure and maybe even bankruptcy. Many have succeeded, but a minority have failed, so research the costs and invest in the assets that fulfill your values.

Tailor Your Portfolio to Your Military Pay and to Your Pension

Moshe Milevsky's book *Are You a Stock or a Bond?* (see Bibliography, page 178) suggests that veterans on active duty can invest much more aggressively than many civilians. Milevsky's concept of "human capital" grew out of his studies of investment and retirement plans. He noted that every worker has the lifetime potential to earn different amounts of money, with varying degrees of reliability and predictability, depending on their potential occupations. Some careers had a high degree of continuous employment and steady income. Civil servants and university professors could all be expected to graduate from their training into relatively steady jobs which, while not paying large salaries, would earn a steady income with good retirement benefits. The modest yet predictable nature of their income was like a bond.

Other occupations, like Wall Street financier or professional athlete, could generate huge payoffs in bonuses or options, but their likelihood of employment and the reliability of their income could be volatile. They could be laid off during any recession, or a single injury could end their career. Although they would probably earn a much bigger total than more steadily employed professions, their income was not predictable and they might even have to arrange for their own retirements with tax-deferred savings and annuities. The volatile swings of their employment and their income resembled a penny stock.

A veteran's "human capital" has the potential to earn millions of dollars over the years between school and retirement. With every paycheck, their years of training, skills, and experience are converted to investment dollars plus retirement and health care benefits. Even in a combat zone their pay, benefits, and insurance rise to cover the higher possibility of injury or death. A veteran's reliable predictability of employment is the equivalent of a steady stream of high-quality income. It's as good as a portfolio of government bonds.

When you're on active duty you'll enjoy a steady stream of largely predictable income. According to Milevsky, the asset allocation of your investment portfolio can shift to stocks because your human capital already resembles bonds. You'll still need an emergency fund and you'll still want to save for specific goals like buying a home, but you don't need to allocate much money to low-volatility assets like bonds, Treasuries, or CDs. As long as you're on active duty or drilling for Reserves/National Guard pay, you can take extra risks with your investments for an extra 1% per year of returns.

If you're saving paychecks for retirement, or if you're retired on a military pension, then you can take extra investing risks! The income stream of your pension is based on one of the world's highest-quality annuities resembling a portfolio of inflation-adjusted bonds or Treasuries. If you had to buy these bonds to produce the income stream of your pension, it's possible that their value would be greater than the rest of your savings. In that case the majority of your overall investment portfolio, including both your pension and your other assets, would be its bond component. Offset that bond allocation by investing the rest of your portfolio in larger portions of equities and real estate. The compounded extra return over 20 years will greatly increase your portfolio and speed your retirement.

The offsetting component of this financial analysis is its emotional turbulence. While your high-equity portfolio will earn a greater long-term return, it has much higher short-term volatility. If you can sleep at night despite a 25%-decline year once per decade, and if you don't need to convert the assets to cash within five or more years, then you could invest more aggressively. You could rely on the bond-like income stream of your paycheck or retirement benefits while raising your asset allocation in stocks, including small-cap and international equities, to enjoy greater returns.

If you find that an occasional 25% loss causes you enough emotional stress to consider abandoning your strategy at the worst possible time (despite its long-term rewards), reduce your asset allocation of equities until the volatility is low enough to live with. Everyone swears that they're able to tolerate a high degree of investment volatility, but that's generally only true during a bull market. No one enjoys downward volatility, and selling equities at the bottom of a bear market will quickly wipe out those earlier years of extra gains.

If you've used your Reserve/National Guard career to reach retirement with a smaller pension, or if you retired with no pension at all, then consider using a portion of your savings to buy a no-frills annuity that provides a small percentage of your retirement income. (Milevsky's book has more details on the types of annuities and their expenses.) Annuities earned a deservedly bad reputation in the 1990s for their high sales commissions and expenses, but even Milevsky has been impressed by their recent improvements. Insurers have learned a lot about estimating their annuity risk, too, and their products are more likely to be backed by a strong company with adequate assets. An annuity isn't as highly guaranteed as a military pension, but your retirement annuity can support a "basic necessity" lifestyle. Keeping the equivalent of a few years' expenses in money markets and CDs will allow you to ride out the worst of a bear market's volatility while remaining confident that your overall portfolio has the resiliency – and the time – to recover from the inevitable financial roller-coaster.

The "Fog of Work"

This chapter's advice has been distilled from a dozen books and websites on lifestyle and financial management. There are literally hundreds of other books with even more detailed information, dozens of computer programs, and thousands of websites ready to walk us through every step of the planning process. The military's pension and TRICARE systems are great solutions to the retiree challenges of inflation and affordable health care. So, why aren't there more military retirees? Why is this so hard for so many people to accomplish?

By now you're beginning to appreciate that the goal takes dedication, commitment, and time. However, another major disruption to the retirement mindset is the "fog of work."

You've probably heard of Clausewitz's "fog of war," or the veteran in your family spends a lot of time dealing with it. For those who haven't had to study military strategy, Clausewitz wrote one of the classic warfare books. One of his most famous quotes is "All action takes place … in a kind of twilight, which like a fog or moonlight, often tends to make things seem grotesque and larger than they really are." [2]

"The fog of work" is the perfect military metaphor for retirement!

During your working years you're expected to strive to get ahead and to stay alert for opportunities. If you don't act when the time is right, then you might miss a great chance to improve your life or your net worth. If you're not happy with your current situation, then you're supposed to take a step back, calmly consider the pros and cons of change, and make a rational decision. Sounds simple, right?

But when we're at work, most of us are focused on our, uh, work. We're not free to work on something else, either, let alone go part-time. In the rare work moments when our laser-keen focus wanders off task for a second or two, we're just taking a mental break. It's like recess at elementary school, with less running around. All too soon the task at hand (or our sense of duty) puts us back on the job. This routine goes on for hours!

When we're not at work, we're getting ready to go to work or taking care of the errands, domestic chores, or child care that supports our household. At night, when we're slumped on the couch channel-surfing the TV, we're still watching comedies about work or thinking about what needs to be done before another workday. Even if we're raising a family, we're training our kids to, uhm, finish school and go to work.

When we're on vacation, we work at playing. We get away from the routine, have new experiences, and socialize. But this can also turn into a military mission order: Drive that highway. Fish that lake. Hike those mountains. Occupy that beach. It's not a time for thoughtful contemplation – it's turned into a time for going places and doing things. It goes on for a week, maybe even 30 days (woo hoo!) before we stop working at playing and start working at getting ready to go back to work. Woo hoo.

Most of our life is planned around our work. We do a lot of work, whether it's productive or not. But when do we get around to planning our life?

Let's not kid ourselves; what we call "planning" is mostly a series of isolated short-term actions along a random walk toward a vague goal. "Dude, that college campus was so cool, I have to escape this loser high school and go there!" "Hey, I could spend the rest of my life with this person." "Someday I'd like to have a baby." "Hmm, no frappalatté today, I'm saving money." "Hunh, what's this about the TSP's 'lifestyle' retirement fund?"

We're "saving money" to buy a house or to go back to school. Meanwhile we're thinking, "Gotta learn more about the housing market soon. And we're going back to school some day, maybe even next year!" We "plan" to get more training and promotions so that we can earn more money while we do more work. We "contribute to our retirement accounts" so that we can retire some day. (Maybe even next decade!) But no one, not even nuclear engineers, plans our long-term budget to project the cash flow savings and its compounded growth into a specific calendar date when we're going to start school, buy that house, and accumulate enough savings to retire. We're lucky if we spend any of our off-work time on "long-term" planning beyond the next meal or social activity.

Perhaps the common factor in the lack of planning is a **fear** of money. Some people lost money in the stock market and feel that their portfolio has to recover, while others have no idea how much they spend now or how much they'll spend in retirement. If people sat down with financial software, they could put together a net worth summary and a cash flow statement. Many would be less afraid of money, perhaps even surprised at the results. Yet when people determine that their retirement income is higher than their expenses, the response is, "Yeah but...," followed by "What if?" or "I don't want to have a problem with..." or even "What will I do all day?"

The real problem is that people rarely find the time to reflect on these life questions or their finances and almost never make the time to do anything about them. We're too busy working. It's hard to learn about the 4% rule, let alone read life-changing books like *Work Less, Live More* (see Bibliography, page 177). But veterans can achieve a net worth at least double that of most retirees, even without having any idea whether they can retire!

This "fog of work" can continue for months, years, even decades. Maybe work is fun, maybe planning is too hard or even scary, or maybe we're too busy with the daily minutiae to focus on the long-term picture.

But one day something clears the fog for a few minutes. Maybe you go to work for the 6,473rd time and realize, "Whoa, this isn't fun anymore!" Maybe there's no 6,474th time because you've just been laid off. Maybe you have a health crisis or a family emergency and you're not going to "regular" work for a while. Maybe you realize that you have no cash flow, let alone compounded growth. As the fog of work creeps back in around your ankles and up your legs, you appreciate that your current strategy (if you have one) just isn't going to carry you to victory anymore. But you'll take care of that real soon. Then...whoops, the phone is ringing and there's new e-mail. And soon the fog of work envelopes you in a smothering embrace.

So the long-term planning happens sporadically, randomly, and super-ficially – if it even happens at all. No wonder the concepts of financial management and retirement are so foreign, even frightening, to people drowning in a fog of work.

Clausewitz's "fog of war" teaches military commanders to plan, adapt, keep moving, and re-plan. There's never enough information at hand to fully understand the situation. They'll never have enough time to figure everything out, let alone to develop a perfect plan. The longer they delay, the fewer options they'll have (or the enemy will remove those options). The commanders' only solution is to pull their heads out of the tactical situation for a minute, stop hoping for the answer to present itself, and look at the bigger picture to see where they can go. Break free. Go there. Now.

It's the same for the fog of work. People have to find a break from their daily busy-ness to learn how to become financially independent and to review their savings plans. They have to practice living retirement without trying to work (there's that word again!) through a huge catch-up To-Do list. No traditional cross-country family vacation or painting the house or writing the Great American Novel. No aggressive new exercise program or yet another diet or one more online course. Try just "being" for a while instead of "doing." After a two-month sabbatical, how many veterans would be interested in going back to work? If we had enough assets (and confidence) to not return to work, perhaps we'd move easily into parenting, exercising, home improvement, and rediscovering our non-work interests. We'd do whatever we wanted without having to sign a contract or make a deadline.

There's only one solution: whisk away the fog of work. Heads will clear after a couple weeks of naps, long leisurely walks, and family discussions. Instead of worrying about "now" or "dinner" or "tomorrow's meeting," the focus can shift to the future and a plan for getting there. Suddenly there's time to design a budget, to read that Bernstein book on asset allocation, and to analyze a retirement portfolio's Monte-Carlo survival during bear markets. There's time to read an entire Ernie Zelinski book and to finish his "Get-a-Life Tree."[3] Try doing those things on a Thursday night after a 12-hour work-fogged day.

Free of the fog of work, many of us would return to duty after a sabbatical and think, "What a bunch of toxic waste." Retirement planning would be promptly executed and swiftly implemented. No more random walking, just a confident stride to the nearest exit.

In a military career, a good "sabbatical" opportunity pops up during a 30-day leave or after leaving the service. It could happen after retiring from active duty, or after leaving active duty for the Reserves, or even when making a clean break from the uniform. A similar opportunity in a civilian career is after a corporate sabbatical (for the few companies that still do sabbaticals) or a layoff.

Now that you've read this chapter, you can find your own path to financial independence. Break free of the fog of work. Plan your financial future and check it a few times a year. Take as much leave as you can get, or find a way to carve out the contemplative time to make a plan. Figure out what you like to do, what you need to do it, and when you can start. Stay alert to the alternate career opportunities around you – the Reservists who report to your command for active duty, the government employees you work with, or the civilian contractors you encounter every day. They can tell you how to make your own transition. As you travel around the world, learn how other cultures view work and retirement. Observe how people in other countries balance living and working. Ask how you can apply what you see and learn to **your** situation. Stay in touch with shipmates who've made the transition to civilian careers or retirement, and ask for their help in developing your own plan.

8

The First Two Years After Retiring

CONGRATULATIONS: you made it! Maybe you finished 20 years of active duty in a blaze of glory with a farewell dinner, a retirement ceremony with full honors, and dozens of family and relatives. Perhaps you did the same in the Reserves/National Guard along with friends from the civilian office. Or you could have finished military service long ago and your retirement is the capstone of a successful bridge career.

However you got here, everyone is starting over. You may be permanently finished with the workplace or you could just be taking a breather before reconnecting with other work or volunteering. This is a time to restart your life and re-examine all your habits.

Relax and Reconnect

One of the first things you can change during retirement is your time perspective. You're accustomed to seeing the future as the next mission, tomorrow's sortie, the next deployment, 30 days of leave, or the next tour. You could still do that, but you don't have to! This is your chance to develop a new perspective: "the rest of your life." It's a gradual shift that may take a few months to develop.

One of early retirement's pioneers, Paul Terhorst, advises taking "the two-year test."[1] When he was first considering early retirement, he thought about what he would do if he only had two years left to live. What would he change? What would he do differently? But once he was retired, he realized that he and his wife were doing exactly what they wanted to do – they wouldn't change a thing. Now they take the two-year test every six months or so and gradually approach new things.

At first, two years may seem like an eternity! But he and his wife have been perpetual travelers for over 25 years and they've learned not to rush into creating new habits. The first couple years of retirement are one of life's few opportunities to contemplate how you want to spend your time. Two years gives you a chance to appreciate the annual routine and to see how things work out. Don't buzz back and forth with a new "To-Do" list changing everything around you. You have the rest of your life to figure out how you want to do this, so relax, slow down, and contemplate the opportunities.

Your top priority is re-engaging with family, relatives, and friends. You might not just have to figure out the new family routine – you might have to get to know each other again! If you've had a career of long deployments and extra hours on the mission, then your spouse is probably accustomed to being in charge of domestic decisions. That is not going to change just because you can make it your new mission. Your kids may also be a bit suspicious of your new schedule. They may be horrified to learn that you're going to spend all your time with them (while secretly enjoying the attention), but they'll also be a bit skeptical that you'll be able to make the commitment.

Even if you're living alone, the first months of retirement are a great chance to reconnect with relatives and close friends. You have the time to spend a few hours with an elderly aunt or to go out for a meal with your wingmen whose schedules never synched up. There's even time for a trip around the country to give people a chance to congratulate you on your retirement all over again. As you visit with these relatives and friends, pay particular attention to the retirees. How did they make their own retirement transition? What perspective have they developed on the future and their own activities? What challenges did they face? These could be the mentors you'd never find around the military or the office.

The first months of retirement are also time to confront the perpetual question of all retirees: "What do I **do** all day?" The cliché response, of course, is, "Whatever you want to." The difference is that you can spend the time to do it without being rushed by weekend deadlines or fighting the crowds. As you contemplate your morning routine, you'll notice that the neighborhood seems to be evacuating around you. Front doors and garages are ejecting their occupants, families are bustling to load up, car doors are slamming, and the streets are full of urgent rush-hour commuters.

Meanwhile you can plan your day at your own pace. Maybe you're continuing a morning workout habit or you're starting a new exercise commitment. Perhaps you'd rather help the rest of the family get out of the house, do your chores before it's hot, or have your own quiet time enjoying the sunrise – if you're even planning to be up this early. Once the rush hour crowds have reached their destinations, you'll be able to enjoy the neighborhood without rushing.

Remember the hassles and crowds of shopping and errands on a Saturday morning? You don't have to do that anymore. The entire world is open, but it's a lot less crowded at 10 AM Tuesday. You can also break up your day with leisure activities – an hour at the library or a quiet coffee house, a workout at the gym, or just exploring the neighborhood. In the shops and stores, you'll notice that the workers have time to answer your questions or to help you plan a project. (No more competing with six other crazed weekend shoppers before you rush back home to prepare for next week's work!) If you adopt a weekly routine, you may get to know the staff and their work schedules, and they'll get to know you. You might even reacquaint yourself with the people around your neighborhood

Back home it's time to think about lunch or projects or even a short nap. After years of long hours and irregular routines, you may be chronically fatigued. The first couple weeks of your new life may even require an extra hour or two of "catch up" naps before your circadian rhythm resets. Even if your eyelids aren't drooping, there's a blissful pleasure in 20-30 minutes of quiet contemplation of your surroundings. Practice "being" instead of "doing."

The afternoon can be more chores or a reward for completing them. If you spent the morning surfing, maybe you're ready to start errands. Or if you spent the morning on yardwork, you might be ready to escape the heat with a visit to a local museum, an uncrowded movie theater, or lunch with friends. Take your time and enjoy being able to focus on an activity. You don't have to rush back to work and you don't have to burn through the chores so that you can enjoy what's left of your weekend. Once again, perhaps for the first time in decades, it's **your choice**.

If you've been perfecting the art of dodging the commuters, you'll get to your evening's destination before rush hour starts anew. The kids will be out of school, ready to spend quality time with you as they discharge their pent-up energy before homework. The neighborhood will start to fill up with cars again as the morning's evacuation reverts to an evening invasion. It's time to start thinking about dinner and spending the rest of the day with family. The retirement difference is that you have time to plan ahead and really enjoy a creative meal, whether it's fixed in your own kitchen or enjoyed at a local restaurant among a few weeknight diners. From now on, you only have to compete with the weekend crowds if you want to.

Speaking of weekends, they can become a retiree's nightmare if they're not paying attention. There's nothing worse than leaving the house for a few quick errands, only to realize that it's Saturday when you'll be stuck in traffic, crowded parking lots, and long lines. You may no longer need to keep track of every minute (more on that later), but you may find it helpful to keep track of what day it is. This is simpler if you have school-age children or a working spouse, but you may still need to have a calendar in every room of the house or a "day clock" that displays the day of the week instead of the time.

Don't Recreate Your Old Environment

Retirement is a great opportunity to make new lifestyle choices, but proceed with caution. Most people are comfortable with the habits they've developed over the years, and upheaval for its own sake can be more disruptive than beneficial. Family members and friends may also be slow to embrace major changes, especially if those changes will challenge their relationships or impact their own routines. So perhaps Paul Terhorst's "two-year test" is a wise way to avoid trouble.

Another danger of this "opportunity for change" is the risk of recreating your old environment. If your workplace personality thrives on crisis, controversy, and confrontation, your family may not enjoy that lifestyle at home. If your career was a perpetual search for the optimal processes, your spouse or neighbors may not appreciate your "benevolent" attention to their efficiency. And if you spent any time at military training commands, especially recruit training, the kids may not enjoy your new focus on their appearance and deportment. You don't want everyone to feel that you're competing with them or scrutinizing their behavior.

An especially treacherous aspect of retirement is replacing your old responsibilities with new ones. The first few years of retirement are a wonderful time for thoughtful contemplation of how you want to live the rest of your life. You may have been responsible for taking care of people and valuables for decades, but don't thoughtlessly fill your new life with more long-term obligations. You may eventually decide that you prefer to continue your old habits with new responsibilities, but give yourself the time to experiment with other activities that bring you value and pleasure. Retirement is a time for personal growth, not repetition or replication.

There's nothing wrong with taking care of family, friends, and neighbors instead of a platoon or a department. It's very fulfilling to lead a local charity instead of a military command. Serving others is a wonderful way to discover new interests and activities for your own benefit. Enjoy the experiences, but be careful not to drop into the old familiar habits of working long hours, pushing to accomplish the "mission," making personal sacrifices for higher priorities, scrambling from one activity to the next, or even running your own domestic personnel and logistics command. Leave plenty of unstructured time in each day for reflecting on your activities and for discovering unexpected opportunities, even if it's just walking the neighborhood or watching the backyard wildlife. In a few weeks you'll find plenty of ways to fill your time and your "To Do" list. If you're seeking inspiration, jump-start your thinking with Ernie Zelinski's "Get-a-Life Tree."[2]

The following sections show how retirees can inadvertently re-create their old environment by giving themselves new responsibilities at serving others or even by being tempted to rejoin the workforce just "because they can."

Forget About Who You Were: Discover Who You Are

That homily makes a great e-mail signature or bumper sticker, but it also carries a warning to a particular segment of veterans. In the military, especially at the more senior enlisted and officer ranks, it's easy to become accustomed to a certain amount of deference and respect. We've all seen those people surrounded by staffs whose main goal is keeping them happy. They have dozens of others catering to their preferences, seeking their advice, and even laughing at their jokes. Of course we were never like that!

For those who identified with their missions or ranks, retirement can be an unpleasant splashdown into very cold water. Suddenly you're on your own, maybe even alone. No one seems to care how your weekend was, how you want your coffee, or what everyone should be working on today. No one even asks your opinion, let alone scurries off to implement your directives. It's hard to tell that people even miss your benevolent leadership, let alone care anymore what you think. You may feel as if you've lost your identity and purpose.

If you want to keep your identity, you might need to review your reasons for retiring in the first place. But if you want to create a new identity, or find a new mission, then retirement is the opportunity of a lifetime. Humans are uncomfortable with change, and retirement is one of life's biggest changes. But rather than resisting the change and trying to cling to an identity, use your retirement to seek out the identity you want to have and what you want to do for yourself.

A VETERAN'S FAMILY member writes about a parent's retirement. "You need a discussion of the 'freaking out' that I understand to be pretty common among people who've recently retired and find that suddenly no one cares who they are or where they are or what they have to say. My dad felt self-conscious about going to the grocery store in the middle of the day because he was afraid that others wouldn't be able to tell the difference between him and 'old people' who had nothing better to do with their time. Fortunately he got over that. I realize not everyone experiences this, but it seems worth at least a mention as one 'normal' reaction to stepping out of a 20+ year routine – and one that can be overcome."

By the way, don't expect your family to step into the supporting role filled by your former staff and soldiers. Not only will they resist playing that part, but they'll worry that you're not handling the transition very well. They've spent years making sacrifices of their own as you made your personal sacrifices for your own mission and wingmen. Now you have an opportunity to acknowledge their sacrifices by spending your time with them. Don't try to lead them. Instead, let them show you how they want to spend their time with you, and then you can show them how you want to spend your new retirement time with them.

Dealing With "Retiree Guilt"

Your new life may also be complicated by the retiree's equivalent of survivor guilt. Instead of coping with the aftermath of surviving a life-threatening situation, your retiree guilt may be rooted in your new financial independence. How can you sleep in when the rest of your family has to get up early for commuting and school? How can you possibly "play" all day when others are trapped by work? How can you share your joy at the fun you've had during the day when they're dragging home from a 12-hour day?

Much of the syndrome can be handled with discretion, common sense, and good manners. It's probably a bad idea to complain about the household's morning noise, and you don't want to drive by your kid's bus stop with your longboard sticking out of the tailgate. When the family straggles home after a hard day, they'll appreciate a clean house with dinner on the table instead of finding voicemail that you're still on the golf course. Everyone should still have their fair share of chores and responsibilities, but you can score extra bonus points by devoting your time and effort to the necessary tasks that come up when everyone else is rushed or exhausted.

Another way to handle retiree guilt is reminding yourself that you worked your assets off for the retirement privilege. You spent long hours in terrible conditions with lousy food and inadequate rest, even before getting shot at or having to deal with other occupational hazards. You've endured years of deprivation that would make convicts riot in protest. You've earned your retirement and you deserve to quietly revel in your accomplishments. People who question your new lifestyle are welcome to contact the nearest military recruiter to arrange their own cushy deals.

An ugly aspect of retiree guilt is other people's jealousy or even envy. Your family appreciates your sacrifices and no doubt shared a lot of their own. But others may have no idea what veterans have to endure to get to retirement – they only see the benefits you're enjoying without appreciating their cost. They don't want to be reminded that perhaps they could have taken similar steps to live more within their means, to save more aggressively, to pursue more education and training, or to tackle a more challenging occupation. While they may claim that you're wasting your life, they're really afraid that they're wasting their own.

You worked hard for your benefits. Enjoy them. You don't have to flaunt your lifestyle, but you have every right to live it the way you choose without hurting others. And in the next section, you can start asserting your "retirement rights" by deciding how you'll choose to spend your time.

Volunteering for Charity or Neighbors

New retirees have the time to sort out their options and to settle on their new lifestyle, but they're still learning how they want to spend that time. However many charities and nonprofit corporations have become experts at recruiting these inexperienced retirees (and their hours of "spare time") to their (usually unpaid) service. This may not be a bad idea if it's part of your plan. Hopefully you considered volunteer service as part of the months of thought and discussions you've had with your family and friends before your retirement.

The good part of volunteering allows you to reconnect with family and community through a fulfilling mission. The challenge of volunteering is that you can easily over-commit yourself and end up rushing among your new obligations. (Just as you used to work long hours on your military missions.) If you've been volunteering with an organization before retirement, this is a chance to become even more involved. But if you've never worked with a particular group before – or never even had the time to volunteer – then move slowly and do your research. Think about how you'd like to spend your time and why you want to volunteer. Look at the group's website and annual reports to see how their money is spent. Talk to other volunteers, especially those who've moved on to other activities and can speak freely about their old organization. Watch other volunteers to see how they're being treated. Visit a charity's offices to get an eye-opening glimpse of their staff and their work. See if they offer "free trials" or if they'll let you work with them an hour or two a week before you make a bigger commitment. You don't want to leap in and then discover that you're burning out on something less rewarding than you expected.

ONE EARLY RETIREE couple had a lifelong fascination with home improvement and wanted to improve their skills alongside the professionals. They were also interested in volunteering to help homeless families, so they joined a local group building homes for the homeless.

The organization was well run and the volunteers got along with each other. No workplace politics or personnel rivalries. Tools and materials were plentiful and help was always on hand for learning a new skill or asking questions. Everyone seemed to be doing a good job on the mission.

But despite these advantages, they were surprised to learn that this wasn't what they anticipated. They enjoyed the idea of doing good while learning new skills, but the hours were longer than they expected and the dedicated construction schedule led to conflicts with other family activities. They were also surprised to find themselves offended by the attitudes of the families they were helping. "Indigent" parents were driving to the building site in new SUVs or wearing expensive clothes instead of appearing to live frugally. Their "sweat equity" contributions were minimal and less than cheerful. They didn't appear to be dedicated to taking care of their children or their other possessions, let alone their new home. Experienced volunteers were familiar with this behavior and had become somewhat cynical about the beneficiaries of their efforts. The whole experience was neither rewarding nor fulfilling, and the negatives outweighed the positives.

They moved on to volunteer at other charities and eventually found their niche. They still enjoy home improvement, and now most of that type of volunteer work is done with friends and neighbors.

As you spend more time in your neighborhood, everyone will learn of your new retiree status. It's a great way to reconnect and become more involved with the community, but don't be exploited. It's not uncommon to hear, "Hey, you're retired, you have the time, and you could help us with this!" It's nice to be invited, but there may also be the implication that your retired time is worthless while your skills and experience are always available to help others. They may mean well, but they may not appreciate that you're already busy. From their work-related perspective, they may naively believe that your retirement frees up at least 40 hours a week to help other workers who are struggling to meet their obligations. There's no need to be offended by mistaken ignorance, but set limits and be firm about what you can or can't do. Help as much as you want, but be clear when you need to take care of your own chores or spend time with family. Even after you retire, you still have a right to enjoy your own personal time!

The Inevitable Job Offers

As you blissfully go about your daily retiree routine, you'll be blindsided by an epiphany: "Gosh, I could do THAT job!"

The realization could be triggered by anything – a clerk's fumbling efforts at the home-improvement store, a chance encounter with a battle buddy, a news item about an old wingman, or a job posting on a website. The evidence has been there for quite a while, but now for some reason you're thinking about a new career.

It may surprise you even more to realize that you're absolutely right – you indeed could do that job, and you could probably find a prospective employer who'd be eager to have you start tomorrow. It seems intellectually challenging and emotionally fulfilling, it might be fun, and you'd even get paid for it! You have to seize this opportunity before it slips away!!

Stop. Take a deep breath and reflect on why you're suddenly so interested. You're not just an old warhorse getting excited by the call of the trumpets. Your instincts may be correct, but you need to think through the issues.

First, it's always flattering when your potential is recognized. This intriguing opportunity could be nothing more than a validation of all your years of training and experience. It's nice to feel this way, but will paid employment make you happy? Do the satisfiers outweigh the dissatisfiers? Are you willing to trade your newfound freedom and flexibility for the inevitable disadvantages of returning to the workplace?

Second, while you think you want the job, do you "need" the job? Even when you're financially independent there can be a dark suspicion of uncertainty in the back of your mind. Maybe your investments won't do as well as you expect. Maybe the kid's college will cost more than you expected, or you'll have to support an aging family member. You and your spouse want to travel someday and the extra money would be nice. Maybe (decades from now) your own long-term care will cost more than you expected. It's possible that your attraction to the job is a way to resolve lingering financial concerns. However, you don't want to start working again merely to realize that you don't really need the money.

Third, is it fair to you and others to take the job? This is a commitment to an employer and co-workers, not just self-indulgent entertainment. The company had to invest a significant amount of time and effort to attract a candidate who they expect will contribute for years. Consider how you'd feel if you were obligated to the job for at least a year. Would it still be paid entertainment, or would you be regretting your choice every time the surf came up?

Finally, would you be able to do "just" the job, or would your competitive instincts kick in again? Veterans are motivated achievers who find it difficult to hold back. After a few months on the job, would you start working longer hours and bringing the office home? Would you be pushing for the training and experience to get a promotion, and climbing the career ladder all over again? Is this what you had in mind when you were originally attracted to the job?

If the job still looks like a great opportunity, then review Chapter 1 and think through the process from beginning to end. Discuss it with your family and friends, and be ready for a long-term commitment.

HIS PHONE RANG six months and a day after retirement (as soon as permitted by the federal ethics guidelines). A fellow Marine was offering a civil-service position almost identical to his last military billet – nearly the same hours and duties for slightly better pay, and even in the same building. The only major differences would be wearing business attire and teaching civilians.

The offer was a total surprise. There had been no retirement job search, not even a resume, and six months had flown by with no thought of going back to work. On the other hand, it was an extremely flattering offer and an opportunity that wouldn't be repeated.

It took over a day for the buzz to wear off, but then second thoughts kicked in. The money was totally unnecessary since they were already living well within their means. His spouse was still working long hours so this job would bring back the pre-retirement strain to their evenings and weekends. The kids were getting too old for after-school programs but weren't ready for the responsibility of coming home to an empty house. It was going to be a full-time job, so several other retirement projects would have to be slowed or even postponed.

continued

The commute would be just as bad as it was on active duty. Teaching meant being on his feet all day and, frankly, his knees were already wearing out. The training was classified with the usual burden of secure storage, page checks, inventories, and paperwork-intensive manuals. The new boss was an old friend and the co-workers seemed eager to have the help, but civil service meant more bureaucracy and office politics. There would also be a lot less time for surfing.

The clincher was his spouse's reminder that his professionalism (and his competitive instincts) wouldn't let him just teach the class and go home. He'd feel obligated to qualify in every aspect of the training, not just his classes. He'd even end up in the office on evenings (to help students study) or weekends (to help operate the equipment). He'd prepare himself to take over for the boss if required. Before long he'd be back in the same hyperachieving environment he'd retired from, just in a different uniform.

He realized that he was thrilled to be asked, but he lacked the commitment to put up with the inevitable drawbacks. As enjoyable as it might be, there was no compelling reason to take the job and he didn't need to revive the struggle of balancing life and work. It also wasn't fair to burden an old friend or new co-workers with these problems, so he regretfully declined.

Several years (and several more job offers) later, he knows he made the right decision.

Retiree guilt, volunteering, and the inevitable job offers are all tempting choices that appear to co-exist with retirement. But beware of the conflicts, and don't create new problems for yourself or your family. When you were working you may have perpetually struggled with work-life balance, and in retirement you'll continue to struggle to balance these options. The only new skill you may need to learn is the ability to say, "Thank you very much for your generous offer, but I can't accept."

Now that you're aware of the issues, take control of your choices. Avoid drifting from one opportunity to the next. Be alert to how they'll affect your feelings and give yourself the time to think through the situations. While each opportunity seems as if it may never be repeated, you don't have to leap on every unsolicited offer. If you feel uncomfortable in your new lifestyle, or if you want to do more volunteering, or if you think you want to work again, make a plan. Work through your feelings, discuss the situation with your family and friends, and start your own dedicated search. But don't compromise your work-life balance for the sake of the job experience. You may decide that there are other things you'd rather do with your life, so be ready to say, "Thanks, but no thanks."

Small Financial Steps

When you're planning and saving for early retirement, your budget is only an estimate of what you think you'll be spending. You'll adjust your estimate as you get closer to retirement, but once you're retired you'll finally know what you're really spending. It's also natural to keep a wary eye on finances during this huge life change, so you may find yourself hypervigilant of every expense or even worrying whether you missed something. The next few pages list an assortment of minor financial details to consider as you fine-tune your plan.

As long as you're focused on your spending, take the opportunity to review your budget and to reassure yourself that you're on track. A great starting point is examining all of your bills and services. For example, retirees are frequently eligible for discounts on home, vehicle, and liability insurance. Your home may be occupied more frequently, leading to fewer accidents or overlooked problems. Maybe you're driving fewer miles or can shift to higher deductibles. If you're not commuting every weekday, maybe you're ready to drop the roadside-assistance membership. If you're a homeowner, check your property-tax assessment to make sure that it's in line with neighborhood values and that you're getting your homeowner (and retiree!) exemptions. As you go about your weekly routine, ask the stores and businesses about their retiree or veteran's discounts. You may even find discounts and double coupons for doing your business on a different day or at a different time.

Another lifestyle question is whether you still need or want to continue all of your frugal habits, or even start new ones. Does your budget depend on you continuing to be frugal? Now that you have more time, will you become even more frugal? Or will you keep your habits at some convenient level simply because you dislike waste?

When you were working you may have avoided small expenses. Every impulse purchase cost you "life hours" of work that would delay your retirement date. Now that you're in retirement, though, small expenses can be just another part of the budget. If your finances have a good year, you may be able to budget more money for small luxuries or charitable donations. In "not so good" years, these small expenses can be the first spending cuts. The nice aspect of this consideration is that you now have a choice – the Girl Scout cookie sale is an indulgence, not an ER-impacting event. You may even decide to focus only on the big financial issues and not worry about expenses that are only a tiny percentage of your annual spending. Keep an eye on the big recurring life expenses like rent, mortgage payments, utilities, groceries, and dining out. Don't worry about one-time spending decisions under $20 – just track the total amount and stop when it reaches your limit.

When you were saving and investing for retirement, it was much easier to reduce your expenses than to raise your income. The same is true in retirement, but most of the retirement calculators are not able to handle this flexibility. The simplest calculators assume a constant spending over the remaining decades of your life, with perhaps annual inflation adjustments. Advanced calculators may handle economic "consumption smoothing" like the expense of a new roof, replacement vehicles, a kid's wedding, or a fantasy vacation. None of the calculators can model aggressive (yet temporary) spending cuts or decide how to shift expenses from one year to another. One of your biggest retirement advantages is your ability to tailor your spending to your situation. The roof has to be replaced someday soon, but you might be able to keep repairing it for another 6-12 months. You may not be able to do without a vehicle for long, but you certainly have the time to figure out alternate transportation for a few weeks while you're shopping for bargains. If a bear market slashes your dividend income for two or three years, you still have the flexibility to allow spending to creep up temporarily, perhaps even as high as an annual rate of 5% or 6%, while you figure out how to reduce expenses over the long term. And if your retirement timing is fortunate enough to enjoy several years of a bull market, you could consider "taking some off the table" to raise your "emergency reserve" and "fantasy vacation" funds.

When you were working, you did some chores or activities a certain way at a convenient location because you had a limited amount of free time.

Now that you're not working, all of those lifestyle choices can be reviewed. A retiree's time and labor are among his/her biggest resources and a great way to avoid "convenience" expenses. If you enjoy cooking, your grocery bill may drop as you buy fewer convenience foods and more raw ingredients. (Of course, you may also spend more eating out!) If you've been using a yard service or house cleaner, perhaps you will decide not to continue it in retirement. It may seem a little silly to go to the gym for a workout when you're paying people to burn at least as many calories cleaning. If you enjoy gardening, you could start growing food and spices along with the landscaping.

Your new daily routine could lower your utility bills. If the house has been closed up all day while you're at work, you may be able to save during your retirement days by opening windows for natural heating and cooling. You could even ask your local utilities for a complete energy audit of your home. If the landscaping has always needed extra water or maintenance, consider changing to different plants. Decide whether to add better home insulation, compact fluorescent light bulbs, insulated windows, low-flow shower heads, Energy Star appliances, and other money-saving improvements. If your home-improvement skills are rudimentary, instead of tackling major projects you could just check for leaky toilets or make sure that the appliances are clean and working well. These tasks may have seemed impossible when you were working, but now your time and your labor are among your most plentiful resources.

You also have the time to become an even more diligent financial manager. You'll already be making minor changes to your portfolio as you shift from accumulating to withdrawals. Now you can research other asset allocations or look for funds with lower expenses. If you've been paying professionals to manage your investments or your taxes, meet with them to figure out what you can do better. Review your record-keeping and deductions and see what changes you can make. For example now that your income is lower, maybe it's worth the tax savings to convert part of a conventional IRA to a Roth IRA. Most retirees have already chosen to manage their own investments without paying a financial adviser. As you become more proficient on your personal tax issues, you may even decide that you can tackle your own tax returns.

Many military retirements involve a change of state residency from your active-duty domicile to your new location. While you're re-registering your vehicles and getting a new driver's license, check with your insurance company. They'll learn about your new residency on their next database update anyway, but they can also make sure you have the right coverage limits or inform you of additional discounts. Now that you're a card-carrying "local," figure out what other discounts you may be eligible for. Your homeowner's property taxes may change. Local parks and museums may have discounted (or even free!) admissions, and local businesses may offer additional bargains.

A few other financial issues may need your immediate attention. As you were preparing to retire, your base's personnel and financial departments should have adjusted your tax withholding. Review that withholding to see if you need to pay more estimated taxes or if you're giving the government too much of your money. If you sold back leave or received other lump sums as you left the service, you may have to pay estimated taxes now to avoid paying a penalty (plus interest) when you file your tax returns. If you're a resident of a new state, your military pension is probably not taxed, but you may still need to adjust your state withholding to make sure that you don't have any unpleasant surprises at filing time. You may also need to consider county or other locality taxes.

When you leave the military, whether by separating or retiring, you have the option to transfer your Thrift Savings Plan. You could roll it over to an IRA or possibly some other tax-deferred investment account, and you could even work out a temporary withdrawal plan to provide additional income until you reach age the minimum age for penalty-free withdrawals. In an extreme case you could even cash it in, after paying heavy penalties and taxes, and use the money for other purposes.

But the best option might be to leave your savings in the TSP. You'll continue to enjoy tax-deferred compounding of your assets up to age 70. Your money is in funds with some of the world's lowest expense ratios, and the fund custodian doesn't use marketing gimmicks or other relentless sales pressure. If you decide to change your asset allocation, you can easily move your TSP holdings among their major asset classes without paying any fees or other penalties. If you retire before the minimum penalty-free withdrawal age of 59½, you may want to consider reducing your future taxes by rolling your TSP account over to a conventional IRA and converting it to a Roth IRA. But you may also be quite satisfied to leave your investments in the TSP until you reach age 70 and then withdraw them as an annuity.

Legislation for the "Roth TSP" is being implemented during 2011-2012. This allows after-tax earned income to be contributed to the TSP. In addition, the Roth TSP feature may allow both conventional IRAs and Roth IRAs to be rolled into the TSP. The TSP's low expense ratios (0.03%) are a very attractive alternative to most IRA expense ratios! Watch the TSP website and newsletters for updates and take advantage of this opportunity.

There is a song by Tim McGraw titled "Live Like You Were Dying," but you may want to invest like you're immortal as you enter the withdrawal phase of your portfolio's financial management. While you were on active duty or in the Reserves/National Guard, you may have cut through the fog of work to decide to put in enough time to earn a pension. Now that you've finally made it, your pension could be your greatest asset because it guarantees a minimum standard of living no matter what happens to your other assets. If you retired without a military pension, perhaps it's worth buying an annuity to pay a guaranteed minimum income during your retirement. Social Security is one annuity, but additional income to ensure a minimum quality of life will help you be more confident about the market risks you take with the rest of your investments. Review the "Tailor Your Portfolio" section in Chapter 7 and decide whether an annuity is appropriate for your situation. Assess this decision every few years during retirement.

There are other ways to create a lifetime stream of income without consuming your principal. A riskier alternative to annuities is dividends from either prefered stocks or common stocks. When you were earning a military paycheck and saving for retirement, you were probably investing aggressively and seeking strong growth from your equities. Growth stocks still have a place in a retiree's investment portfolio, but you might be more comfortable with a steady stream of dividend payments to complement your pension.

During a bear market, another way to prolong your portfolio's survival is to stop withdrawing from it until it recovers. If you choose to maintain a high asset allocation of equities during retirement, then ensure that you have enough spending cash to ride out downward market volatility and the recovery from a recession. (Nobody worries about upward market volatility!) While you were earning a paycheck, you were confident that you'd be able to replenish your emergency funds in a few months. You were also setting aside savings for short-term goals like a new vehicle or the down payment on a house. In retirement you need to keep at least a year or two of savings in cash to pay your expenses if your portfolio drops 25-30%. (Even retirees still need to set aside funds for short-term goals like a new vehicle or replacement household appliances.) Most bear markets have lasted for two years and some have been even longer. Many retirees keep their cash reserve in CDs to pay a minimum of two to five years of expenses beyond those covered by their pension and investment income. Tailor your own cash reserve to your comfort level, your asset allocation, and your willingness to seek part-time or short-term employment. You can also spend down your principal if you expect it to last for the rest of your life. But if you're blessed with unexpected longevity and no longer able to hold a job, then your only other option would be to cut back your lifestyle to live within your pension.

If you elected to have survivor benefits paid on your pension, review this arrangement every few years to ensure that it meets your beneficiary's needs. You can't change your military pension's survivor benefits, but you can consider additional life insurance or change the asset allocation of other investments.

A word of caution about maintaining your retirement investments: don't make it any harder than you want to. You don't have to be an investment guru unless you want to be one. You may have the time to spend hours day-trading futures contracts, but you shouldn't do so unless you find it fascinating or entertaining. Picking individual stocks may seem like a great way to generate extra spending cash, but it also requires a considerable commitment to research and tracking. Only a small fraction of investment professionals are able to beat their market's returns, and there's no reason to expect that you'll be able to do so without investing at least as much of your time as your money. Even if you are able to beat the market, it's hard work and it requires continuous effort. Maybe you're wondering if you're the next investment genius to beat Warren Buffett's record, but he exerts a tremendous daily effort on research and analysis that borders on obsession. If it seems like the life for you, then take a small percentage of your assets – 5 to10% – and explore your curiosity to your heart's content.

WHEN I TOOK early retirement, I was confident of my investing abilities. After all, I'm a highly trained veteran who's spent over half my life making quick decisions with incomplete information under life-threatening stress. I wasn't going to spend the rest of my life wondering how good I was – I was going to find out while I still had my sentience and courage, and I'd dispassionately benchmark my accomplishments against the professionals.

When I inherited a few thousand dollars, I set up a brokerage account with all the features: real-time streaming quotes, low commissions, fast execution, margin loans, options leverage, and everything that Wall Street (and the Internet) can provide to us retail investors.

Over the next five years I read and researched for several hours a day while working through all the investing styles. I educated myself and tested my mettle through day-trading, momentum investing, value investing, technical analysis, penny stocks, microcap stocks, commodities, real estate investment trusts, initial public offerings, limit orders, stop-loss orders, automated quantitative-analysis trading systems, shorting, options, and a whole dictionary of stock-picking acronyms.

Experience proved to be a quick and brutal teacher with expensive tuition. Surprisingly, each year I got a little better. My analytical and critical-thinking skills improved. I learned how to read financial reports and arcane SEC filings. I studied accounting analysis. I learned how to build spreadsheet models of revenue and cash flows. I caught several trends and made huge short-term capital gains in some stocks while getting savaged in others. I made better choices and fewer mistakes.

During the fifth year it all came together, leaving me with a difficult decision – continue the experiment or take my profits? One choice made itself when valuations went from "high" to "nuts" and I cashed out. I looked for other undervalued stocks, but everything seemed richly priced. It was time to start shorting the market.

I abruptly realized that I was no longer enjoying myself. I'd learned a tremendous amount, and I'd been able to (eventually) apply it

continued

with extremely gratifying results, but I was spending 20 hours/week on research. I was also tired of tracking the positions and dealing with the daily stress of the critical details – and there were a lot of critical details.

When I analyzed the short-term results with my latest picks, I saw that I was barely ahead of the market. I was winning the race, but I was running hard to stay ahead of the pack. Over the five years that it took me to accumulate sufficient knowledge and experience, I'd only managed to beat money-market returns. Meanwhile, a stock index fund would give me market returns with a tenth of the effort. I elected to return to index funds so that I could enjoy more time with my family – and more surfing. I haven't completely quit stock-picking, but I don't let it become a time-consuming job.

Healthy Lifestyle

Now that you're financially independent with more control over your time, it would be a shame if this "retiree duty" ended early from negligence. One of your new goals should be to maximize your longevity!

Turn that goal into a plan and execute it. After years of denial and deferred gratification, it's tempting to spend all day in front of the TV with junk food and beer. You've earned it, right? When you were in the military, your chain of command ensured that you maintained a minimum level of physical activity. In retirement, however, you have to take responsibility for your own health and fitness. The good news is that you can always fall back on group exercise or a personal coach, and now you have plenty of time to try all those lifestyles and activities you've been curious about.

When you finished your military retirement physical, you may have found issues that wouldn't delay your retirement but needed your corrective attention. Blood pressure and cholesterol levels may have been rising over the years along with body weight, and you may even be on corrective medication. You're probably already coping with two occupational hazards: too much stress and too little sleep. Retirement gives you a chance to figure out long-term solutions for all of these problems.

Many retirees report that their first months of retirement included dramatic reductions in stress, weight, and blood pressure. Instead of eating on the run or binging on fast food, you have time to redesign your routine, restock the house with healthier food and snacks, and eat smaller meals at more regular intervals. Instead of going on a diet, a lifestyle solution would be to move to a better cuisine. This is your chance to explore a high-fiber, low-fat menu, more raw ingredients, fewer convenience foods, different cooking styles, and new recipes. Instead of trying to get going each morning with caffeine or energy drinks, you could focus on a wake-up routine that includes better hydration and a more leisurely breakfast. Instead of "lunch hour," you could balance your body's digestive activities (and insulin levels) with smaller meals and more frequent snacks. Instead of racing home at the end of the workday to gorge on dinner and collapse in front of the TV with "dessert," you can add an afternoon workout or an after-dinner walk and still have plenty of time to cook. Now that you won't be trapped on watch or in meetings, you can drink as much water as you need and even use the bathroom whenever you want!

As you recover from years of chronic fatigue, think about what physical activities you want to enjoy for the rest of your life. Decades of government-sponsored exercise and operations may have ground down some body parts, especially knees and backs, while age may also be making inroads on your physiology. You no longer have to design your exercise around passing the next physical readiness test, either. You could continue sports and activities that you've been enjoying for years, or you could explore new ones. Try to select a variety of ways to improve strength, coordination, flexibility, reflexes, and aerobic fitness.

After retiring, when you first visit a doctor (for whatever reason), look around the waiting room and consider how your life has changed. When you were in uniform, doctor's visits may have occurred all too frequently as an interruption to your workday. In retirement they may happen annually or even less often, and you'll have to make the most of that time with research beforehand and a list of questions. Instead of having to squeeze the appointment into your workday or field maneuvers, you can arrange a convenient visit when both you and the doctor have time to talk. If you're at a military clinic, take a look at the patients in uniform – you used to rush around with that look on your face, too. While your vital signs are being checked, you can chat with the assistants instead of hustling through to the exam. You could even let them know that you've recently retired and ask them to compare your previous heart rate and blood pressure readings for improvement. The doctor needs to hear that you're retired, too, so that you can check for the inevitable physiological changes and evaluate whatever treatments you may be continuing from active duty.

As you move toward a healthier lifestyle, take the time to make a gradual long-term change instead of punishing yourself with a "training camp" or dietary deprivation. You don't have to rush it, and you want food and exercise to complement a new routine instead of disrupting it. You can't abruptly cut off the caffeine or immediately switch to a high-fiber diet or suddenly train intensely for a triathlon. Your body will not cooperate with the change, you may even risk injury, and your suffering will kill your motivation. Research, experiment, and progress slowly. Make lists of the things you want to improve and consider planning them out on a calendar for the next 6-12 months. Build up your strength and your conditioning while your body adapts to your new diet. Make one or two gradual changes a month instead of slamming yourself into a new regime. Gradually ramping up to next year's 10K road race is much more achievable than trying to cram in double workouts for next month's Ironman Triathlon.

Here's a final note about taking care of yourself. Once you're officially retired, register at your local Veteran's Administration office and consider making them your primary care manager. One critical reason to register with them is to enable them to quickly notify you of any veteran's health issues that you may have unknowingly been exposed to in uniform. Another good reason is to document your local residency, which lets them claim their fair share of funds to support the veterans in their service area. Federal and state governments have also invested a lot of effort and money to improve the VA's offerings and the quality of their service. Older veterans have a certain impression of the agency that may no longer be accurate in your area. You may find that their primary-care management is even better than a civilian clinic, and they have a much better appreciation for military occupational hazards or other lifestyle issues.

Rebel a Little

Now that you're taking better care of yourself, it's time to have fun with it. While you're designing an improved lifestyle for yourself, you can also get a life.

It bears repeating: retirement means that you're responsible for your own entertainment. This is especially true if you happen to have retired at a more senior rank, where you had a team devoting their efforts to meeting every one of your goals and keeping you happy. That lifestyle is over! While your spouse and family are happy to have you back in their lives, they may not necessarily share your new-found joy at being the focus of all your time and attention.

Luckily you can creatively think up plenty of entertainment. You can also evaluate all of your workplace-survival tactics and decide whether they're still necessary. For example, are you wearing a watch? Why? When you were at work or on duty, it may have been necessary to coordinate your activities down to the second, but do you need to continue that? It's a tiny step to put your watch away for a few days, but it may require a big leap of faith in yourself. At first you'll find yourself walking around to find a clock, and you might even have a momentary panic of "I'm late!!" But for what? After a few weeks you may have stopped looking for clocks. By the end of the first year you'll know as much about the time as you care to, but you'll be looking for a calendar to figure out what day it is.

Do you have to make your bed every morning? That may have been important when you were experiencing reveille and inspections, but those days are over. No one is going to care about your hospital corners, and you'll probably be back in bed in a few hours anyway for an afternoon nap. Sure, it'd be nice to set a neat example for the kids, too, but no one has to stow for sea anymore. Maybe the younger ones would share the thrill of your retirement by not having to make their beds every morning, either. Years later you may still feel as if you're getting away with something.

Navy veterans of a certain age may remember that sad 1980s day when beards were outlawed by the uniform regulations. (Don't worry, submariners, your secrets are safe with me.) Men felt that it was nice to shave less, beards kept faces warm during cold weather, and a few shipmates' chins desperately needed a well-groomed coat of hair. If you're now a retired man, what better way to remind yourself than by growing a beard, or at least a goatee and sideburns? The shock value with family and friends is priceless, and you can decide one last time if growing it is worth the itchy phase. Even if you shave it off again after a month, you can still relax your former clean-shaven standards. Shaving twice a week will keep you groomed enough and, if done regularly, it can help you remember what day of the week it is.

Speaking of hair, when was your last haircut? For at least the last two decades you've had little or no choice about your hair length and style, let alone its color and accessories. Once again you have a new opportunity: your hair could be the longest it's ever been. You won't have to put your hair in a bun or braids unless you want to. (Guys, this applies to men as well as women.) For some of us it may be the last chance to discover what our hair can do! If you're a parent, few things will annoy your kids more than experimenting with your hairstyle. They'll happily complain to their friends about the phase their parents are going through, but secretly they'll be impressed and looking forward to their own retirement.

You get the idea, and from this point you can let your imagination run wild. Tattoos and body piercings are no longer out of the question, either, although you may still feel compelled to set an example for impressionable teens. Others may see retirement as a chance to have a tattoo or two removed without worrying about inappropriate workplace attention.

While you're enjoying a little rebellion, remember to keep it "little." Retirement is a fantastic opportunity to experiment with alcohol, smoking, or even riskier behavior. Family and friends don't have to know about this research, and you don't even have to worry about military urinalysis! But as you start this new phase of your life, the last thing you want to do is to risk your health (or your arrest record). In extreme circumstances you might risk your longevity, not to mention your military pension and benefits. There are hundreds of sad stories of retirees who couldn't be responsible for their own entertainment and turned to riskier behaviors out of boredom or even fear. That's not rebellion; that's avoidance and defeat. You've looked forward to retirement for decades and you've been preparing for months. Turn your lifestyle **healthier**, not more hazardous.

Where Do You Want To Go Next?

You might have joined the military to see the world, but now you can do it all over again at your own pace.

Vacation travel is expensive on a fixed schedule for short times at destination resorts. Retirement travel and perpetual travel can exploit seasonal prices with longer stays. If you're qualified for the military's space-available flights, travel is even more affordable. Hotels and vacation condos can be negotiated at discounted rates for extended stays, and it's easier to rent private apartments or homes for month-to-month visits. "Living local" avoids resort prices for food and transportation while exploring undiscovered attractions off the tourist track. Rural and overseas locations have significantly lower expenses to support the perpetual traveler's lifestyle. Recreational vehicle travelers can stay on the road for years and may no longer even maintain a house. See the Recommended Reading section on pages 181 and 188 for more guides and websites, especially from the Kaderlis and the Terhorsts.

Don't be surprised if you're restless after a year or two of retirement. Veterans may initially find it unusual or even uncomfortable to live in the same place for more than two years. Like it or not, you've become accustomed to the transfer cycle of moving in, unpacking, settling in, then a year or two later saying "au revoir," cleaning out your excess possessions, packing up the rest, and moving on. Frequent moves force families to have fewer possessions or responsibilities, and their change of address becomes its own routine. Now that you're retired you'll easily acquire all sorts of new furniture, hobby supplies, recreational gear, or even pets. Suddenly your home is full of possessions and you need a major clean-out just to be able to store it all. Meanwhile, after two or three years you begin to notice your "Why are we still here?" attitude. It may even feel like time to "move on" or to try a new location.

When that feeling creeps up on you, acknowledge it and "move" beyond it. Spend a family evening with the photo albums reminiscing about those transfers. Talk about the old decisions and compromises, remember what went well, and think about the future. You may even be shocked to realize that it's been two years of retirement already, and that you can have many more here. You won't have to get restless anymore, especially when you can travel as much as you want.

What about "back to school"? A surprising number of retirees seek out the classroom, especially if they feel obligated to extract every penny from their GI Bill benefits. Some see school as an opportunity to make up for lost time – the education they could never afford or the training that always seemed to take too long. Others go back to school for the chance to learn new skills or to advance their degrees. A few even go back to school to avoid boredom and make productive use of their time.

Just like a job offer, consider the reasons that additional education is suddenly so important to you. If this has been your life goal for decades and you finally have the time and money, then enjoy yourself! Explore your curiosity while you're still motivated to succeed with the educational bureaucracy. You'd be setting a great example for your family, especially your kids. You could be on the road to a doctorate, a new career, or even an avocation.

BOXKICKER (from Chapter 1) is back with an update. Financially independent on his pension yet with very little savings, he decided to semi-retire and pursue his graduate degree while working part-time as a starter at his local golf course.

"I am finishing up my bachelor's degree using the Montgomery GI Bill (MGIB). I have already taken one course and my final course will leave me with 34 months of benefits. I am going to continue my master's degree through our state university using MGIB's Chapter 30 vice Chapter 33 (Post 9/11 GI Bill) because I am going to do it online. Under those programs I'll take a course every two months for 24 months at a total state resident's tuition cost of $9,900. During that time the Veteran's Administration will pay me almost $24,000! Even after finishing up my master's degree, I will have more benefits remaining via the MGIB and even more under the Chapter 33 benefit.

"The reason this works so well is that I was nearly finished with my bachelor's degree when I retired. I'd strongly encourage all veterans to get as much of their education done on active duty (using Tuition Assistance funding) before retiring. Now it's paying me handsomely!"

Be sure to understand why you're interested in returning to school. If you're using school for the structure and socialization, then you may want to reconsider your commitment. At first it's comforting to know that you have someplace to go at 9 AM Tuesday, but as the months go by you may begin to resent the constricting routine. School is not as confining as the cubicle environment, but it's still an environment with assignments, deadlines, and performance reviews. Making the time for homework, projects, and exams may be more of a burden than you care to handle.

The socialization may not be what you expected, either. The student demographic could be much younger than you with much less world experience. The students with full-time jobs won't be interested in spending hours delving into every detail of the material. Others may be busier with family priorities, leaving you to feel that you're handling too much of the group assignment. You may be enjoying knowledge for its own sake while others feel the competitive pressure to excel, maintain their scholarship, or even qualify for better jobs or salaries. There will be an ever-present temptation to cut corners or even ignore a rule – not quite the ethics you may have been expecting.

Are you seeking educational wisdom to make up for missed opportunities or because you need more credibility? If you're still smoldering with resentment that the military never sent you to graduate school, or frustrated that your deployments always conflicted with your course requirements, then you might want to re-evaluate your reason for working so hard to get through a program that may only lead to an awards ceremony. Your advisers and fellow students want you motivated by the desire to learn, not by a desire to avenge old wrongs. If you feel that you need a degree or certification to validate your existence, imagine how you'd feel spending months or years on that goal. During your working years it might have been important for certain duties or jobs, but do you need it for your retiree life? Will your family, relatives, friends, or neighbors care that you have a master's degree or a CPA certificate?

Part of your feeling of obligation may be caused by a desire to make the most of every opportunity. If your military benefits didn't offer the program, would you still try to go back to school? Earlier versions of veteran's educational programs were "use it or lose it" and had to lead to a definite degree or certification before the deadline. If you don't need to achieve a certification, then the program may not retain your interest. The latest version of the GI Bill actually allows beneficiaries to transfer their benefits to spouses or children. Would you rather give your opportunity to someone who could change their life more than it would improve yours? The transfer flexibility can make it less urgent to jump back into the education and training routines that you maintained in the military.

If you've ever been an instructor at a military training command, and most especially if you've ever been in charge of evaluating instructor techniques, then be very careful about your decision to return to school. Your teaching knowledge and experience make you one of the world's worst students and a professor's nightmare – a fellow professional instructor. You'll be so distracted by different teaching styles and errors that you'll have trouble following the material, and the instructor will soon grow to dread your every question and comment.

If you don't "need" the degree or the certification, and if you're not "wasting" a benefit or some other opportunity, then you don't "need" to go back to school. Learning for knowledge's sake is always a good idea, but the structure and the deadlines can turn an enjoyable experience into a painful marathon. Instead of subjecting yourself to the traditional academic environment, why not create your own program? Many schools and colleges offer local residents a chance to monitor or audit courses without the requirements of assignments or tests. You may not be allowed to ask questions or join in group activities, but you have a no-obligation chance to read the books, sit in on the teaching, and enjoy the show. If a higher priority comes up, then you're not skipping school or letting down your classmates. You can tailor your learning to your personal needs – for example, you may not need to complete every course of an accounting degree to be able to manage your own investments.

You might even be able to teach yourself from books and websites. Instead of going "back to school," you could create your own "school," tailored precisely to **your** needs and on **your** schedule. If it doesn't work out the way you expect, you can always fall back on your military benefits and the educational system.

Going back to school may be the right choice for you – it certainly was for "Boxkicker." He planned ahead and worked hard on his bachelor's degree before he retired from active duty, so he was ready to start his master's degree and maximize his GI Bill benefits. His degree will fit right into his new part-time occupation, and sports management may turn out to be his avocation. He completely understood what he wanted to do and how to do it. Make sure that you understand your own goals and motivations before signing up.

Retirement is the best time of your life for change, but don't be disruptive. It may also be the first time that you've ever had so much control over so many aspects of your life, so take it slowly and give yourself (and your family) plenty of time to adapt. Don't give up that control, and don't drift along letting change control you. Think through each of your changes and consider whether you'll see the commitment as an incentive or a burden. Give yourself time to adapt to each change, to decide whether it's temporary or permanent, and to learn whether it supports or interferes with your other change plans. Don't burn out. You have the rest of your life to experiment and enjoy your changes, so don't make things happen so quickly that retirement becomes painful.

9

The Future

THE END OF THE retirement fairy tale: *"And they all lived happily ever after."* Right?

You Will Change. Your Plans May Change Too.

Not so fast. If you retire in your 40s, your demographic can look forward to a minimum of 30 years of being responsible for your own entertainment. For financial-planning purposes you should count on 40 or even 50 years. You'll find plenty of things to do all day, but each day will present its own set of challenges.

It's quite possible that you'll evolve as a human and your priorities will change. Retirement may turn out to be your avocation, but if you encounter another type of avocation, you should feel free to pursue it. Retirement is a life-changing event, and the subsequent years will change you too.

Long-term Goals

If you're the type of person who keeps a list of very-long-term goals, here are some longevity events to tackle:

- Stay healthy and active longer than the median of your demographic
- Join the list of the 10 oldest alumni from your schools or military occupations
- Collect more pension checks than paychecks (bonus: correct the totals for inflation!)
- Discover your "dream avocation"
- Teach your family's next generation(s) how to achieve retirement

When you build your own list of long-term goals, visit one of the retirement websites in the Recommended Reading section on page 188, and share your list with the rest of us!

Find Your Avocation?

When you started planning your retirement all those years ago, your top goal was to leave the workplace as quickly as possible – probably with the financial independence to never have to return. You'll have enough money to avoid the workplace for the rest of your life, but don't lock yourself out of the office just for the sake of maintaining your independence.

After a few years of retirement you may find yourself reflecting on your ideal avocation. Many of us achieved retirement through an occupation (like the military) or a series of jobs and never found our true avocation. Maybe your avocation offers a fulfilling sense of accomplishment, total creative control, and a flexible schedule. Maybe there are no bosses, other employees, office politics, long hours, painful commutes, or workplace uniforms. Or perhaps you'll discover the traditional corporate ladder of your dreams and begin climbing to your heart's content. Your goal is to achieve the financial independence to spend your retirement time as you see fit, and to be able to change your life without fear of poverty or deprivation. Maybe retirement is the only avocation you'll ever want, but you should also devote your time and energy to pursuing your dreams.

Another benefit of financial independence is seeking the work you truly love. You have to love it, because you're rarely getting paid for it! Most retirees find this through nonprofits, whether by becoming an employee of an agency or by volunteering where they see fit. The beneficiaries of your efforts are what make your work so fulfilling. You can focus your efforts locally or at making life better for all of us. While you may enjoy delivering your personal touch at a shelter or school, you can also help an advocacy group to campaign for better health benefits for the homeless or to call attention to veterans' legal issues.

You gain creative control just by agreeing to tackle a job that's been languishing. Anyone who interferes with your control also risks the chance that you'll simply drop the job and move on, leaving the organization with another vacancy. It's the same for a flexible schedule – the organization appreciates that some of your time is better than none at all.

If you find your avocation, it won't even feel like work. If you're getting paid for any of your efforts, you wouldn't mind donating all of it to charity. Your intangible rewards are worth far more to you than the effort or the money, and you're honoring a debt of appreciation owed to those who helped you find your path to financial independence.

Paying it Forward

There's nothing wrong with seeking your avocation by trying different types of work or volunteering. But you can simply enjoy "not working" for the rest of your life! You've earned your retirement, and you have no further obligation to society beyond living a fulfilling life that does no harm. Working and volunteering are just two aspects of life, even if they're part of a perpetual search for your avocation.

As we get older and reflect on our accomplishments, our attention begins to shift to the next generation and our legacy of "paying it forward." You had many mentors and benefactors who looked out for you when you were younger. You may have been able to pay them back with more than your sincere thanks, but in most cases we feel obligated to those who helped us, even at those times when we didn't think they were helping. Now that you have plenty of retirement flexibility, it may be time for you to consider how you'll repay the largesse of those who helped you. One of the best ways to do that is to pay it forward to the next generation by mentoring someone who needs it as much as you did. Whether you do that through teaching at a college or volunteering at a local school or just spending time with family, you may be able to pass your retirement skills on to the next generation.

Another way to pay it forward is to talk about retirement. Join an Internet discussion board or start your own website or blog. You may not find many retirement fans among your relatives or in your neighborhood, but there are plenty of attentive readers on the Internet. This book was conceived from several of those websites, and dozens of other early-retiree readers helped bring it to print.

But if you don't feel the motivation, you don't have to work or volunteer, or even mentor. Financial independence and retirement give you the right to enjoy your life as you see fit! Live your life as the example you'd like others to emulate – you'll be both mentoring **and** paying it forward.

"WHO ARE YOU WITH?"

An alumni class was having their 55th reunion in our city. My spouse and I volunteered to staff the hospitality suite for a rare opportunity to see a snapshot of the lives of those who'd gone before us. What a great chance to see veterans and long-term retirees in action, and to learn from the experts!

We met people about whom we'd only read – heroes of the Korean War, the Vietnam War, and decades of Cold War history. Many had gone on to successful civilian careers. We also met their spouses and families and heard dozens of fascinating unpublished stories. It was wonderful to get to know these harbingers of our own aging, and an inspiration for reflecting on our own lives.

My spouse and I, in our 40s, had been asked by several attendees how we found the time to volunteer on a weekday morning. We explained our military careers and our early retirement, despite their disbelief and warnings of certain boredom and lack of fulfillment. We soon dropped the subject – this demographic was not the right audience for a discussion about early retirement.

One alumnus stood out from the other more flamboyant and voluble attendees. He was of modest stature and seemed reserved, even shy, but he possessed a room-commanding presence. His voice had the timbre and echo of professional speech training, and his words were full of credibility and experience. It was observed that he'd flown cross-country to spend this time with his classmates, even as it took him away from a ceremony at our alma mater. When pressed, he admitted that he'd just been honored as one of its distinguished graduates.

He seemed familiar but his name didn't spark our limited memories. (We certainly didn't share his social or professional contacts.) Later we read much more about his impressive military career and his even more outstanding accomplishments in the corporate and nonprofit worlds. He had accumulated much recognition and many awards. He was certainly financially independent and thoroughly

continued

enjoying his avocation. His legacy would be reflected in histories, museums, and monuments. His contacts and recommendations would open doors of opportunity across the nation in military and corporate circles. To be blunt, he was the job-seeker's employment reference of a lifetime – a fantastic networking contact!

While he'd been talking with the group, he'd also been observing my ponytailed enthusiasm about surfing and our family's early-retirement lifestyle. During a late-morning lull when my spouse and I were alone with him, he asked me, "So, who are you with?"

My reflex response was, "Why, I'm here with my spouse." (My spouse thought he wanted to know who brought us to the reunion.) As my confusion showed, he clarified, "With what company are you working?" I quickly reassured him that I was delighted with early retirement and not seeking employment. After a few skeptical questions he accepted my position (without understanding it) and moved on to other topics.

Later that night, as my spouse and I learned his biography and discussed our conversation, it became apparent that I'd stumbled into the job interview of the century – and totally blown it. I was absolutely oblivious to the rare opportunity he'd offered and blissfully ignorant of its significance. It was the clearest sign yet of how thoroughly I had been enjoying early retirement.

Conclusion: Enjoy the Journey

There are many paths to retirement, and there are many paths to explore during retirement. You worked hard at your military career, and you had to work even harder to build your assets. You endured frugal sacrifices that may not have been supported by friends, let alone relatives and family. Simply choosing your retirement lifestyle may have exposed you to society's criticism and even jealousy.

Once again, you've earned it. Harvest the fruits of your labors and enjoy the journey through whatever paths this book helps you choose. If retirement leads you to your avocation, then pursue it just as enthusiastically as you pursued financial independence and retirement. If **retirement** turns out to be your true avocation, then keep looking forward to exploring each new day. Now that you're financially independent, you should experience your life. Don't just get through it!

APPENDIX
A

Effect of Inflation on a Dollar

The following graph shows the corrosive effects of inflation over four decades. The lowest rate, 3%, is approximately the average rate of inflation over the 20th century.

The highest rate, 5%, is the approximate average inflation rate over 1970-2000. These years are notable for the 1970s oil embargo and 1973-4 stock market crash, as well as the October 1987 stock market's one-day drop of 25% and the 1990s run-up of technology stocks. Annual inflation rates reached double digits in the 1970s-80s and required extraordinarily aggressive intervention by the Federal Reserve to return inflation to "historic" levels. During one year of this time, military pensions even received two cost-of-living-adjustment raises in the same year!

Early retirees have to consider the effect of inflation for two reasons. First, they will spend a significantly longer time in retirement – as much as 40 years – and during that time will see inflation erode their original early-retirement dollars to as little as 13-30 cents. The COLA in a military pension goes a long way toward neutralizing inflation.

The second important point about inflation is investment asset allocation. Only one asset class has historically beaten inflation over the long run of 20-40 years of retirement: equities. An early retirement depends on multiple streams of income from pensions, Social Security, and investments. Most early-retirement survival projections expect to consume at least a portion of the early-retirement investment portfolio's principal and not to just live off dividends. Early retirees cannot hope to keep up with inflation by investing their portfolio in only TIPS or I bonds. The length of retirement will exceed the maturity of the securities, and there's no guarantee that replacement securities will be readily available when the portfolio expires. TIPS do not include a portion of their inflation adjustment until final maturity, and the Treasury restricts the amount of I bonds that individual investors can purchase each year. They'll either need to reduce their lifestyle to stay within the income of their pension/Social Security or to assume greater market risk (volatility and loss) by investing in stocks.

There's one other aspect of inflation to consider for service members tempted by the REDUX retirement system. One "feature" of a REDUX retirement is that COLA increases are 1% less than the CPI. That doesn't sound like much of a loss next to the prospect of receiving $30,000 five years before retiring, but the reality is that it equates to 1% higher inflation for at least 20 years of retirement. The difference between 3% inflation and 4% inflation for 20 years amounts to 10 cents out of every early-retirement dollar. After the first 20 years of early retirement, a $20,000/year REDUX pension loses over $2,000/year every year over a High-Three pension and, throughout an early retiree's lifetime, will add up to far greater losses than the prospective gains of the $30,000 REDUX bonus. See Appendix D (Effect of Inflation on a REDUX Military Pension) on page 160 for more details.

Average inflation rates and historic stock returns are obtained from Dimson and Marsh's *Triumph of the Optimists*. See the Bibliography on page 177 for more information on this book and other investment information.

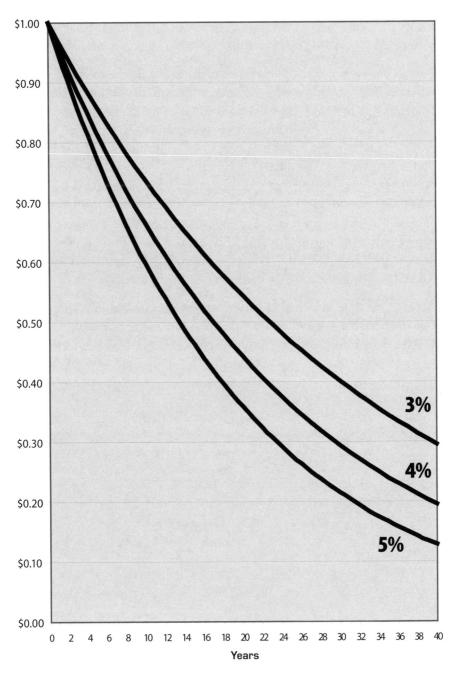

Effect of Inflation on a Dollar

B

Saving Base Pay and Promotion Raises

Retirement dates are accelerated by saving as much as possible in the Thrift Savings Plan, IRAs, and taxable accounts. Aspiring early retirees have two ways to boost their savings: earn more or spend less.

Military earnings rise with each new pay table, longevity raise, or promotion, but it's all too easy to let lifestyle spending take over the higher income. The raises in each year's annual pay tables generally go up at the rate of the Employment Cost Index, hopefully keeping up with inflation but rarely exceeding it. Just boosting TSP contributions by the annual pay increase is not enough to attain early retirement.

Aggressive savers should invest as much as possible of both their base pay and every promotion's pay raises while holding their spending below the previous pay grade. Saving for early retirement would be easy if an E-7 could hold the expenses of an E-1, but this is unrealistic. (It's deprivation, too!) A more achievable E-7 goal would be holding spending at the pay grade of an E-6 and banking the pay difference between E-7 and E-6.

The graph on page 152 shows how quickly that savings can compound. It uses the 2009 pay tables and assumes that military pay keeps up with inflation over a 20-year career. It assumes reasonable promotion rates for E-2 through E-7 and O-2 through O-5. It also assumes that the servicemember saves 10% of their base pay at one pay grade below their current rank, and 80% of their pay raise from their latest promotion.

Savings are invested over 20 years and compounded at a conservative 3% over inflation in the TSP, IRAs, and taxable accounts. Three percent over inflation is a reasonable rate of return for an investment portfolio concentrated at least 80% in equities.

The assumed promotion ranks with years of service when promoted to that rank (see table on page 153) may vary by service and specialty.

Saving base pay and promotion raises

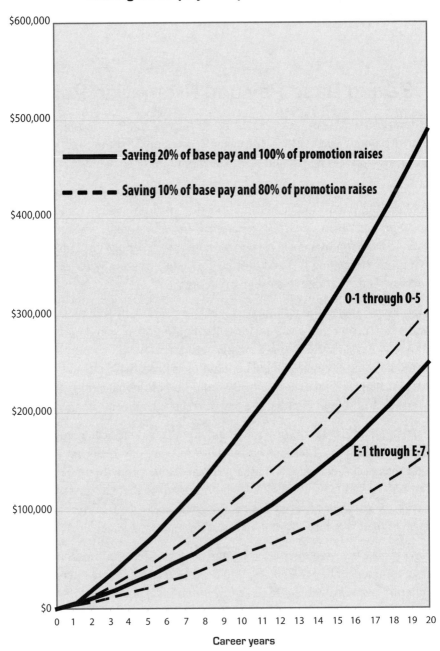

Rank	Years of service when promoting to that rank
E-2	1
E-3	2
E-4	4
E-5	7
E-6	10
E-7	16
O-2	2
O-3	4
O-4	10
O-5	16

The military pay tables include raises for both longevity and promotions, so members earn longevity raises every 1-2 years in addition to promotion raises. However, these savings assumptions don't include the longevity raises, so veterans will be able to use longevity raises for spending – or additional savings.

An example of the savings goals for an E-5 in year 9 of their career in as follows: Their promotion to that rank occurred in year 7 and they're attempting to live as though they were still receiving E-4 pay. They're saving 10% of E-4 base pay and 80% of the pay raise (between E-5 and E-4 pay) from the "over 8 years of service" column of the pay table.

The following year (year 10), that E-5 is promoted to E-6, but the graphed results conservatively assume that the pay raise takes effect at the end of the year. Their longevity hasn't changed because they're still over 8 years of service but not yet over 10. So the same "over 8" pay scales are in effect and the member is saving the same as in year 9.

The year after (year 11), the recently promoted E-6 uses the "over 10" column for E-6 and E-5 pay grades. They'd save 10% of E-5 base pay and 80% of the pay raise (between E-6 and E-5 pay) from the "over 10 years of service" column of the pay tables.

Other conservative assumptions include:

- No money is saved during the first year of a 20-year career, which really hurts from a compounding perspective but is a reasonable fact of life.

- Active-duty military savings and compounding rates occur at the end of each year instead of at twice-monthly paydays.

- Tax-free allowances like Basic Allowance for Housing are not included in the savings rate, allowing them to be used for higher housing and utility costs.

- Special pay and bonus pay are not included, although a frugal aspiring early retiree would save both whenever possible.

The graph on page 152 shows results for two different cases:

1. Saving 10% of base pay (at the previous pay grade) and 80% of the promotion pay raise.

2. Saving 20% of base pay (previous pay grade) and 100% of the promotion pay raise.

Note that a small increase in savings percentage has doubled the size of the final investment, even though the biggest raises occurred late in each career.

The portfolio will grow even faster if additional money is invested from early career savings, longevity raises, higher allowances, special pay, and bonuses.

APPENDIX

C

Retiring on Multiple Streams of Income

CWO2 Jane, age 40, tentatively plans to retire from the Reserves at age 42. She's going to continue working in her civilian career (for now), but she's eager to retire from that, too, as soon as she can comfortably live off her assets and her pension(s).

She realizes that she might be able to completely retire somewhere between age 42 and age 65. Her confidence is boosted by knowing that at age 60 she'll have the Reserve pension adjusted every year for inflation, plus very affordable TRICARE health care insurance.

Jane has spent many hours on her detailed budget. It includes her living expenses and high-deductible catastrophic health insurance before age 60, as well as the replacement costs of vehicles and major appliances. She's even added in a couple of fantasy vacations and a new roof. She's estimated her property taxes and state/federal income taxes in her 15% bracket, although her military pension is not subject to state tax. She projects a basic budget of $35,000/year, but she'd prefer to have $40,000/year to spend some money on travel and other entertainment.

She just received her Reserve verification that she's served 20 good years with a total of 3,800 points. The maximum longevity pay at her rank is W-2>24 – $4,935/month. Her pension will be based on the military pay scale in effect at age 60, 18 years from her planned retirement date. Assuming that military pay keeps pace with the Employment Cost Index and the Consumer Price Index, in 2009 dollars she'll get a pension (with a COLA) of 2.5% x (3,800/360) x $4,935 = $1,302/month or $15,627/year.

Jane has no idea what future inflation will be, but she knows that the 20th century averaged about 3% per year. She estimates that her COLA will be the same as the CPI. To be conservative, she'll estimate that her spending will also rise at the same rate as the CPI. (For the purposes of this example, it keeps the results in equivalent inflation-adjusted 2009 dollars. A retirement calculator or a spreadsheet will be able to handle different rates of COLAs and inflation.) She knows that she could also cut her spending to her basic budget.

In addition to her Reserve pension, Jane also has $250,000 in taxable accounts. Her conservative mix of stocks, bonds, and cash pays a long-term average of 5% per year, although that fluctuates +/- 10% from year to year. Since inflation is rising at 3.5% per year, she knows that her taxable account's after-inflation "real" return is only 1.5% per year, and she still has to pay taxes on its gains when she withdraws the money. These taxes are part of her basic budget.

Jane's civilian employer does not offer a defined-benefit pension plan – only tax-deferred investment accounts like a 401(k) or a 403(b). She has $75,000 in her tax-deferred accounts, including the military's Thrift Savings Plan. These accounts can generally be tapped without penalty after she turns 59½ years old, and she must begin required minimum distributions shortly after age 70. She can also make penalty-free withdrawals using the Internal Revenue Service's rule 72(t) system of "substantially equal periodic payments." Because she doesn't have to pay taxes on these accounts until she withdraws from them, she's hoping to let them compound their tax-deferred earnings as long as possible. She's invested these accounts in more volatile assets such as equity indexes in small-cap value and international stocks. She expects to receive a long-term result of 7% per year, or 3.5% per year after inflation (and before taxes).

Jane has another $100,000 in her Roth IRA; $50,000 is from her 20 years of after-tax contributions. She can withdraw her contributions anytime without penalty, and she can withdraw the earnings without penalty after she turns 59½. Again, she's hoping to let this account compound its tax-free earnings as long as possible because it's also invested in volatile assets and will hypothetically reach a higher value.

Jane is entitled to Social Security as early as age 62 (at the time of writing). If she starts distributions before age 67, though, they'll be permanently reduced by as much as 25%. She plans to delay receiving Social Security until at least age 67 and, if possible, age 70. Based on her current earnings record and the Social Security online calculator, at age 62 she'll receive $1,050/month ($12,600/year), at age 67 she'll receive $1,400/month

($16,800/year), and if she can wait until age 70 she'll earn $1,700/month ($20,400/year).

Jane begins by estimating her lifetime annual income if she retires at age 42:

Age	Income	Shortfall	
42	$0	$40,000	
60	$15,627	$24,373	From Reserve pension only

At this point she'd need $40,000/year to maintain her ideal lifestyle. Although her $250,000 taxable account may continue to grow at 5%, $40,000/year is an unsustainable withdrawal rate. If it continues to grow at a steady 5% per year, then it might last seven or perhaps eight years. However, a bear market could cut her to less than five years, even if she drastically reduces her spending.

If she depleted her taxable investments by age 48, then she'd turn to her Roth IRA and her tax-deferred accounts. Her Roth contributions would give her another year of penalty-free withdrawals to make up her shortfall, but then she'd have to start withdrawing the rest of the accounts (through a 72(t) SEPP plan). (SEPP stands for Substantially Equal Periodic Payment.) The tax-deferred accounts would have grown during the years that she was spending down her taxable assets and her Roth contributions, but she'll almost certainly deplete her Roth IRA and her 401(k)/TSP before her Reserve pension begins. That's not going to work.

She realizes that her retirement is in jeopardy between ages 42 and 60. But when her Reserve pension starts, will she have enough for the rest of her life? Conventional wisdom (from the Trinity Study) claims that she can begin withdrawing up to 4% annually of her remaining assets (and raise that amount every year for inflation) for 30 years.

Age	Income	Shortfall	
60	$15,627	$24,373	Reserve pension only.
62	$28,227	$11,773	Reserve pension and a 25% reduction in Social Security benefits.
67	$32,427	$7,573	Reserve pension and full Social Security.
70	$36,027	$3,973	Reserve pension and maximum Social Security.

A shortfall of $24,373 at age 60 requires a portfolio of $610,000 to support a 4% withdrawal rate ($24,373 divided by 4%, or multiplied by 25). However, by age 62 she only needs a $295,000 portfolio to support the shortfall on a 4% withdrawal rate, and by age 67 it's under $200,000.

At age 42 Jane will only have $425,000 in assets, but she can see that by age 62 she'll have more than enough to retire even if she doesn't save any more in her taxable or tax-deferred accounts. If she continues working (and saving) for the next 18 years, she'll be able to retire at least by age 60, when her Reserve pension starts.

There's a safe haven between the two extremes: (1) retiring from both the Reserves and her civilian job at age 42 and consuming her investment portfolio, or (2) working until age 60 and retiring on several streams of income. The simplest option would be to continue serving in the Reserves and her civilian career until her portfolio is big enough to bridge the gap. Even another five years of Reserve drills would add at least 375 points to her total and 10% to her pension. Another option might be to invest a portion of her portfolio in rental real estate to generate additional cash flow, although landlording involves additional risks. A conservative option might be to continue her full-time civilian career and Reserve drilling for another 5-10 years before retiring from one, and then consume her portfolio until her Reserve pension starts (with employment income and enough portfolio left to make up the shortfall). A fourth option would be working part-time, or on a series of temporary jobs, to allow her to semi-retire and enjoy some extended travel before age 60.

Jane can fine-tune her retirement date by running spreadsheets and retirement calculators. (See the Recommended Reading section for websites and other products.) The biggest factor under her control is maximizing the amount she saves in her tax-deferred and taxable accounts. Another factor is gradually reducing the equity risk of her taxable account when she gets ready to spend it; she doesn't want to have to liquidate it in the middle of a bear market. Finally, staying healthy is a big incentive to reduce the cost of health insurance. She can't do anything about her genes or catastrophic events, but she can maintain healthy habits and avoid "lifestyle" syndromes like tobacco or weight gain.

In this example, Jane could afford to retire in her mid-50s and perhaps even in her late 40s. Her situation is a simplified version of real life. Real-life planning becomes much more complicated when raising a family, paying a mortgage, and saving for a child's college education. It becomes even more difficult if a divorce, a stock-market meltdown, or prolonged unemployment derails the plan. The key to success is deciding what brings value to life – spending money or saving it for retirement. There's a balance between the two, just as there's a balance between a Reserve/National Guard career and a civilian career.

APPENDIX
D

Effect of Inflation on a REDUX Military Pension

Veterans entering the service after July 1986 are eligible to choose between two different retirement systems. The first system, High Three, offers a multiplier of 50% at 20 years of service and raises it 2.5% per year to 75% at 30 years of service. Each year after retiring, the pension is raised by a Cost of Living Allowance (COLA) that's an estimate of the previous year's increase in the Consumer Price Index (CPI). This COLA is intended to keep up with inflation, which the government typically measures with the CPI.

The second retirement system, REDUX, starts its multiplier at only 40% but raises it 3.5% per year to 75% at 30 years of service. It also includes a COLA, but the COLA is capped at 1% less than the CPI. When the retiree reaches age 62, his/her REDUX pension is "reset" to the value it would have reached with a full COLA. After age 62, though, the COLA returns to its cap of 1% less than the CPI.

The biggest difference between the two systems is the Career Status Bonus (CSB) paid during the 15th year of service to veterans choosing REDUX. If the entire after-tax amount of the bonus is invested and the veteran stays on active duty long enough, then under certain optimistic assumptions their total CSB and REDUX pension lifetime value will be greater than if they had opted for the High Three pension without the CSB. At most ranks and years of service, though, the High Three's full COLA grows faster than the CSB can compound.

Even worse, every year the CSB loses ground to inflation. Ten years after the REDUX system was modified, the CSB is still $30,000. Even if inflation was only an average of 3%, Appendix A (on page 148) shows that a decade of 3% inflation has already reduced the "real" (inflation-adjusted) value of the CSB by over 25% since the law was passed. As military pay and pensions continue to rise, inflation will continue to erode the CSB and make it less valuable to a REDUX retirement.

The Department of Defense REDUX calculator is difficult to evaluate because it does not adjust its numbers for inflation. The graph below is based on a spreadsheet that adjusts each year's pensions (both High Three and REDUX) for inflation. If the CPI equals the actual rate of inflation, then the High Three pension's COLA keeps up with inflation and the inflation-adjusted value of the High Three pension stays constant. The REDUX CPI, however, is capped at 1% below COLA. The inflation-adjusted value of the REDUX pension loses 1% every year until age 62. At age 62, the REDUX pension is reset to its original inflation-adjusted value. After age 62, though, the REDUX pension again loses 1% per year for the rest of the veteran's life.

The graph assumes that the REDUX retiree invested his/her entire after-tax REDUX bonus ($25,500) in a mutual fund yielding a realistic 3% after taxes and inflation. The invested CSB compounds for five years before both veterans start their pensions at age 38.

At retirement, the REDUX retiree starts with a lower pension ($15,576/year instead of $19,470) but an inflation-adjusted CSB value of $30,448. He has more money than the High Three retiree until both are 46 years old, when the High Three retiree's total pension pulls ahead. The REDUX reset at age 62 slightly reduces the widening gap but by age 70 the High Three retiree has received 17% more money – nearly $100,000.

The Department of Defense's REDUX website shows several case studies for different lengths of service and ranks. Other military-media websites have additional criticisms of the REDUX system and its effect on veterans who don't clearly understand its risks. See the Recommended Reading section for more links.

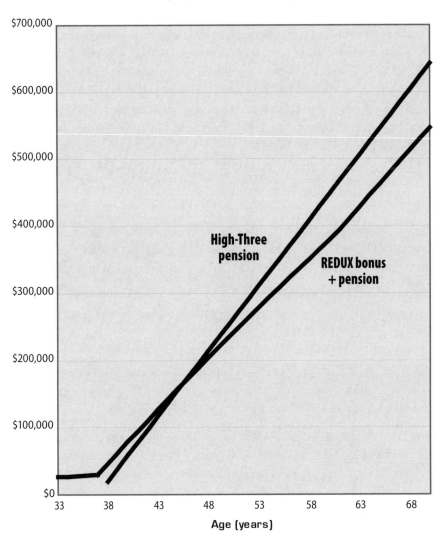

High-Three pension versus REDUX bonus + pension
(adjusted for inflation)

APPENDIX
E

"Present Value" Estimate of a Military Pension

How much is a military pension worth?

The answer is more than just cash flow. Another way to ask the question is: How much is that pension worth as a lump sum?

Humans aren't very good at estimating income or inflation adjustments, and emotions will always influence our otherwise logical financial decisions. Unfortunately an investment that looks like a great deal in a glossy magazine ad can turn out to be "great" only for the seller. A very effective way to analyze a pension's value is to put the numbers in terms of both the pension's monthly cash flow and its lump-sum equivalent.

The answer's format can change a veteran's decision. The Department of Defense still offers a REDUX Career Status Bonus because many military members (and their families) are tempted by a "big" number like $30,000. But Appendix D showed that the CSB is usually only a good deal for the DoD.

At first glance a military pension doesn't seem to be worth very much. Even a relatively large pension of $3,000/month is about $100/day. Soldier just ending their 10th year of service might not be very motivated by the thought that they'll have to work another 10 years for that guaranteed cash flow of inflation-protected income. Emotionally, $100/day just doesn't seem worth the sacrifice, even though the payout rises with inflation for the rest of their life.

The challenge behind analyzing a lump-sum question is to figure out how much money has to be invested to yield the pension's stream of income. One problem with the analysis is that the military pension includes a cost of living allowance (COLA), so the amount of the income stream has to rise every year by the rate of inflation. Another problem is that no one knows how long the pensioner will live, so it's difficult to predict how long the pension will be paid out. Finally, the lump sum has to be invested in a safe and stable asset, such as Treasury bills, to make sure that it survives for decades. Unfortunately the safe and stable assets have a very low yield, so it takes a larger lump sum to produce an income stream big enough to pay the pension.

The answer to all of these puzzles involves the mathematical process of "discounting." Accountants and actuaries devote entire careers to studying asset yields, human longevity, and other risks. They calculate the statistical probability that a certain lump sum will be able to pay a particular pension for the necessary number of years. The good news for pension recipients is that the calculations are much more accurate when the analysis is simultaneously applied to hundreds of thousands of pensions as a group. Even better, the Department of Defense can rely on the number-crunching skills of another giant bureaucracy of inflation-adjusted payments: the Social Security Administration.

The mathematical details of discounting an inflation-adjusted annuity are well beyond the scope of this appendix. There's not an easy formula to convert that $100/day pension to a precise and accurate lump sum. However, there are a few simpler estimates that are reasonably close to the more complicated methods.

The easiest estimate assumes that a military pension keeps up with inflation. This eliminates the more complicated factors of correcting future dollars for inflation. If a military pension keeps up with inflation, the pension's value in today's dollars stays constant. The lump-sum value of the pension is the total amount to be received during the rest of the veteran's life:

Lump sum = (annual pension amount) x (remaining life expectancy)

A 38-year-old veteran receiving $3000/month with a COLA might reasonably look forward to 35 more years of life. The estimate of the present value of their pension would be:

Lump sum = ($3,000/month) x (12 months/year) x (35 years) = **$1,260,000**

The life-expectancy estimate ignores other discounting factors in favor of simplicity and speed. Its main advantage is that a veteran can quickly estimate a lump sum for their own personal expected lifespan. Veterans in good health with long-lived ancestors may decide that they have 40 or even 50 years of retirement, raising the current value of their pension.

Another quick estimate is to assume that the pension is the income stream from a lump sum of Treasury Inflation-Protected Securities (TIPS). TIPS are an extremely safe and stable asset with built-in inflation protection. The market for buying and selling TIPS is huge and liquid, so their prices are fairly accurate. One flaw of this estimate is that, unlike a military pension, when the pensioner dies there's still a lump sum of TIPS generating a stream of income. Another drawback is that the maturity of a TIPS (currently a maximum of 20 years) is usually less than the pensioner's remaining life expectancy. The advantage of this estimate is simplicity and speed:

Lump sum = (annual pension amount) / (TIPS annual percentage yield)

A January 2009 Treasury auction sold 20-year TIPS at an inflation-adjusted annual percentage yield of 2.5%. So, for that $3,000/month pension,

Lump sum = ($3,000/month) x (12 months/year) / (.025/year) = **$1,440,000**

Another estimate of the lump-sum value of an inflation-adjusted pension is a commercial annuity. The annuity market is generally regarded as liquid because insurance companies compete with each other to offer the "best" price without losing money. However, they still charge more than the actual value of the annuity to make their profit. Insurance companies could be unable to make annuity payments or even go bankrupt and should be considered a riskier source of annuity payments than TIPS or other government bonds.

One of the "less risky" annuities comes from an agency sponsored by the federal government – the Thrift Savings Plan. TSP annuities are actually purchased from an insurance company and are not guaranteed by the federal government, but the insurance company is presumably charging a smaller fee (t o sell a large volume of annuities) and the annuity's cost would be closer to its actual value.

TSP annuities are priced each month and do not offer full protection against inflation. The advantage of estimating a pension's lump-sum value from a TSP annuity is its lower price and the TSP website's calculator.[1] Assuming that the $3,000/month pension is paid to a 38-year-old veteran and limited to 3% annual inflation:

Lump sum (TSP website annuity calculator) = $1.4 million

The $1.4 million total is the actual fee that a veteran would pay in the market to purchase a TIPS portfolio or an annuity that would yield their inflation-adjusted pension of $3,000/month for the rest of their life. Other research [2,3] analyzes the theoretical cost of annuities and discounted values – only the cost and not its actual market price. These estimates range from about $1 million to $1.2 million. They're only theoretical estimates. These annuities can't actually be purchased like the assets of the other estimates, but they're a more conservative estimate of the probabilities of longevity and other risk factors.

Let's get back to the veteran who's just finished 10 years of service and is wondering if it's worth staying in the military for another decade. After an analysis of the pension's present value, which option sounds more compelling now: $100/day or a lifetime income totaling over $1 million?

APPENDIX
F

Asset Allocation Considerations for the Lump-Sum Value of a Military Pension

There are two aspects to every financial decision: the logical and the emotional. Both aspects are equally important, and investors who make their decisions based on just one aspect will find it very difficult to stick with their commitments. Investor psychology research into "loss aversion" has shown that a loss of money causes far more pain than a gain of the same amount.[1] Even if an asset-allocation plan is chosen with the most rigorous criteria and extensive analysis, the inevitable periods of high volatility or unexpected losses can cause far more pain than the benefit of any gains. That emotion can overcome rational thinking. Investors eventually accept that the most logical and well-researched asset-allocation plan is useless if they're not also emotionally comfortable with the results. When the markets perform badly, even for a short period, distress can cause investors to sell out (and lock in their losses) at the worst possible time. This path to retirement is long and painful.

One distress-free option would be to invest in assets that have no volatility and never lose money. Treasuries, TIPS, and I bonds all attempt to offer this solution. One drawback is that these "risk-free" investments pay a very low rate of return (sometimes no return at all) and Treasuries can actually lose value to inflation. Their low yield means that it also takes much longer to save enough to support even a frugal lifestyle. Even when a portfolio is big enough for its returns to support retirement, it will only keep up with the Consumer Price Index (CPI). If a retiree's rise in personal spending exceeds the CPI, they risk outliving their assets as their personal inflation erodes their value.

A high-stress option would be to embrace volatility. Many investors spend months researching the mathematics and histories of asset allocations. They become experts on the correlated performance among different classes of stocks, bonds, real estate, commodities, and cash. The idea is that when one asset class is performing poorly, another asset class will be rising at least as quickly to offset the overall portfolio. Nobel-winning researchers have been able to "prove" that a diversified portfolio built from uncorrelated asset classes is actually less volatile than the individual assets in that portfolio.[2]

Unfortunately the diversification "proof" only works most of the time, not all of the time. As the recession of 2008-09 showed, the markets are still not efficient. Low-correlated asset classes can still drop together for days or even weeks before investors stop selling and are tempted to buy. "Portfolio insurance" methods can minimize the impact of these rare episodes, but their expense reduces the portfolio's overall return. Spending hundreds or even thousands of insurance dollars a year (on stock options that expire worthless) seems like folly in the heat of a bull market.

Another option, dividend investing, is a variation on a diversified portfolio of volatile assets. Investors own shares of diversified yet high-yielding stocks. They plan to receive enough dividends to live off the portfolio's yield without ever selling any shares. This plan works well in a bull market because companies generally strive to please their shareholders by raising dividends even when their shares are growing in value. In bear markets, a company will avoid cutting its dividend whenever possible in order to pre-serve shareholder faith (and its share price). Long-term investors can look forward to years of dividends that hopefully meet or exceed inflation while never having to worry about volatility or selling shares in a bear market.

A minor drawback to dividend stocks is that their share price tends to grow more slowly than the rest of the market because their yield is a larger part of their total return. Another issue is that it takes a larger portfolio of dividend stocks to support retirement expenses. Instead of spending principal, a divi-dend portfolio can only support a withdrawal rate of its total dividends – usually 2-3.5%. The portfolio never runs out of money since principal is never consumed, but it takes longer to save enough to support retirement.

Unfortunately the 2008-09 recession also showed that companies will cut their dividends to avoid bankruptcy. The stocks of financial companies (banks and investment firms) were hit particularly hard, with some even cutting their dividends to a token penny a share.[3] Dividend-paying stocks are an important part of a diversified portfolio, but dividend stocks should not be the only component of a portfolio.

A final option would be to sidestep volatility and render it irrelevant. It requires saving enough cash (money markets and CDs) to support living expenses during a bear market. Investors live off their cash while they wait for the bear market to end and their assets to recover. This works well for all but the longest bear markets. Although investors can ignore downward volatility for months or even years, the emotional impact may still be severe enough to make them question the wisdom of this asset allocation.

Most investors choose a middle ground among the various investing options. Savings are invested in assets whose returns are expected to beat inflation. Diversified portfolios assume risk with volatile assets, but the assets are split among several classes to reduce overall volatility. A portion of the portfolio is also kept in cash to support living expenses during bear markets. The relative amounts of these assets are chosen not only for their inflation-beating mathematical interactions but also to allow investors (and their spouses) to enjoy a good night's sleep.

Even with this accumulated wisdom, investors are still trying to put the 2008-09 stock market meltdown in perspective. It's painful to watch equity portfolios go into free fall, even if a diversified plan minimizes the paper losses. When asset classes fall below the portfolio's allocation, it's a great opportunity to rebalance by buying more shares at a discount. The portfolio's cash allocation provides the spending money to ride out a bear market while waiting for the rest of the assets to recover. But the emotional depths of a bear market can still make even the most dedicated investors question their logic and their discipline.

One economist's perspective compares an investor's portfolio against their overall lifetime income. Moshe Milevsky's book *Are You a Stock or a Bond?* describes the "human capital" of lifetime earnings and pensions. Although savings are important to retirement, the size of an investment portfolio may be a minority of a retiree's net worth when compared to their lifetime earnings power and their pension income. Military retirees, with their stable incomes and high-quality inflation-fighting pensions, can have a particularly high human capital – outside of a combat zone.

"Human capital" is also a good career perspective. Veterans tend to be paid less than their civilian counterparts (while getting shot at more often), but their employee benefits are at least as generous and their likelihood of continued employment is much higher. Milevsky's book uses the examples of university professors and Wall Street stockbrokers. Professors make far less each year but (with tenure) can look forward to a lifetime of paychecks. Stockbrokers may earn millions in one year but could be unemployed the very next morning. Their high-dollar earnings power has very little to do with any guarantee of continued employment. The challenge for both occupations is to manage their spending (and their savings) at an overall level supported by their salaries, no matter how low or uneven their income may be.

Human capital is a relatively new concept and not yet widely accepted. Most financial analysts and website calculators ignore human capital by treating salaries and pensions as "just" a stream of income and not considering their impact on a portfolio's overall asset allocation.

Military retention is another impact of human capital. At some point every one of 1.4 million veterans (and their 1.9 million family members) has to decide whether or not to stay on active duty or to continue drilling in the Reserves/National Guard. Only 15% of the military's members stay on active duty for at least 20 years. A pension is not the only reason to stay on active duty, but it would certainly help people endure long, dangerous deployments or stressful midwatches. The military may be a familiar lifestyle with a guaranteed paycheck, but is it worth the pain? If human capital could compare the earnings of active duty to the Reserves/NG, or assess the impact of completely quitting the military, then the analysis could bring financial logic to an intimidating lifestyle decision.

"Net worth" doesn't account for cash flows like pensions or Social Security, so their income has to be included as their lump-sum equivalent. A convenient assumption about inflation-adjusted pensions is that their payout is constant in today's dollars – they maintain their buying power for the rest of the retiree's life. So, like the first estimate of a lump-sum pension in Appendix E, the value of an inflation-adjusted pension is related to the owner's life expectancy. Other methods in Appendix E can give a conservative range of estimates of the pension's lump-sum value.

Reserve/National Guard pensions and Social Security are more complicated because their payouts start later. However, Congress and the Department of Defense attempt to improve retention by raising military pay at least as fast as inflation, while promotions and longevity pay keep individual veterans ahead of inflation. It could be assumed that future pay dollars will have the same buying power as today's dollars. The Social Security website's benefits calculator also produces its results in today's dollars, and benefits are adjusted for inflation. That means a Reserve/NG pension and Social Security are paid in inflation-adjusted "today" dollars from their starting point through the rest of a life expectancy.

The lump-sum discounting math is more complicated for military pensions with survivor benefits and for civilian defined-benefit pensions without inflation adjustments. Military-benefits retirement calculators [4] produce enough financial information to allow a rough estimate of the lump-sum value of survivor benefits. Civilian corporations base their pension calculations on actuarial information that allows their human-resources departments to provide employees with an estimate of the pension's lump-sum value, and labor unions or other employee organizations may offer their own analyses.

Once projected pensions and Social Security benefits have been converted from income streams to lump sums, they can contribute to a veteran's net worth. Investment portfolios would be added at their current value, as well as homes or rental real estate. Personal property (such as vehicles, furniture, recreational equipment, and clothing) can also be included. Mortgages, vehicle loans, and other debts are subtracted to get the total net worth.

The results can be startling. Investors have been admonished to save their money and invest in a diversified portfolio of stocks, bonds, cash, and perhaps real estate or commodities. A number of investment companies offer "balanced" funds, and the TSP offers "lifestyle retirement" funds that adjust their stock/bond asset allocation to a target retirement date. However, all of these methods ignore an investor's human capital of their pensions and Social Security. Appendix E showed that the lump-sum value of a $3,000/month military pension is at least $1 million. This inflation-adjusted pension is paid by the federal government from Treasury securities that have zero risk, so it's the equivalent of an extremely high-quality bond portfolio. An investor with a $250,000 investment portfolio split between stocks and bonds may think that their stock/bond asset allocation is 50/50. If the $1 million lump-sum value of a military pension is added in, the actual stock/bond allocation is 10/90! [5] Even if the portfolio loses half its value, the loss of net worth is not 50% but rather 10%.

Other researchers have found similar imbalances for retirees whose Social Security benefits have skewed their asset allocation almost as heavily toward bonds.[6]

How should veterans use this information? How does it affect their decision to stay in the military? How can the lump-sum value of their pension and Social Security benefits affect their asset allocations?

First, veterans have to consider their human capital in their decision whether to leave the service or stay until retirement. During a 20-year career it's possible for enlisted to earn over $1 million in pay and benefits, and officers to earn twice as much.[7] Money should not be the most important factor in a retention decision, but it is significant.

Second, military veterans can assume more risk (returns and volatility) in their investment portfolios. Their likelihood of continued employment is higher than most civilian occupations and their human capital is distributed more evenly during their careers. Their asset allocation could be more conservative if they leave active duty for the Reserves/NG or quit the military entirely, but during active duty they can invest more aggressively.

Third, a military pension is probably a veteran's most valuable asset. As a high-quality bond, it allows investors to move the rest of their investment portfolio heavily into stocks or other assets. If loss aversion causes emotional distress during a bear market, the paper losses in a stock portfolio can be considered a small percentage of the retiree's net worth. Their pension and Social Security are inflation-adjusted assets that are far more significant, even if a stock portfolio loses half its value. Veterans (and financial advisers) have to consider the lump-sum value of these benefits in designing investment plans and asset allocations.

Chapter and Appendix Notes

Chapter 1

[1] The term "bridge career" comes from Marc Freedman, the author of *Prime Time* and *Encore*. It describes whatever work a person does between retiring from their first job and fully retiring from all paid employment.

[2] *America's Military Population*, by David R. and Mady Wechsler Segal. The percentage of retirees from each service varies widely, with the Air Force retaining as many as 30% of its personnel for at least 20 years.

[3] "A Comparative Study of the Life Satisfaction of Early Retirement Military Officers," doctoral dissertation by Russ T. Graves, professor at Texas A&M College, 2005.

Chapter 2

[1] Philpott, Tom, "Retired Pay Differences Rise," 27 March 2008, *Military Times Publications*. http://www.military.com/features/0,15240,164817,00.html?wh=benefits

[2] "Retirement Savings: Choosing a Withdrawal Rate That is Sustainable," by Philip L. Cooley, Carl M. Hubbard, and Daniel T. Walz, professors of finance in the Department of Business Administration, Trinity University, San Antonio, Texas. Published in the *AAII Journal* February 1998, Volume XX, No. 2, of the American Association of Individual Investors. One of many public links to this article is at http://bobsfiles.home.att.net/trinity.htm. A more detailed analysis is at http://assetbuilder.com/blogs/scott_burns/archive/2004/06/01/Portfolio-Survival_3A00_--Income-Trumps-Diversification.aspx and http://www.retireearlyhomepage.com/novtips.html.

[3] William Bernstein, "The Retirement Calculator From Hell," part III, archived at http://www.efficientfrontier.com.

[4] Clyatt, Bob, *Work Less, Live More*, 2005.

Chapter 3

[1] *Cashing in on the American Dream: How to Retire at 35*, by Paul Terhorst, 1988. More information also at http://sites.google.com/site/paulvicgroup/.

[2] *The Adventurer's Guide to Early Retirement*, by Billy and Akaisha Kaderli, 2009, download from http://retireearlylifestyle.com/orderpage.htm.

Chapter 4

[1] Some veterans are concerned about recording their DD-214 as a public record because it contains their Social Security number, which would then be publicly accessible and a risk for identity theft. For others it reveals more information about a military career than perhaps you would want available for public inspection. You may decide that the risks of identity theft and adverse publicity are not worth the convenience.

Chapter 5

[1] *America's Military Population*, by David R. and Mady Wechsler Segal.

[2] "Retirement Savings: Choosing a Withdrawal Rate That is Sustainable" by Philip L. Cooley, Carl M. Hubbard, and Daniel T. Walz, professors of finance in the Department of Business Administration, Trinity University, San Antonio, Texas.

[3] *The Millionaire Next Door*, by Thomas J. Stanley and William D. Danko, Simon and Schuster, 1998

Chapter 6

[1] *America's Military Population*, by David R. and Mady Wechsler Segal.

[2] "Retirement Savings: Choosing a Withdrawal Rate That is Sustainable" by Philip L. Cooley, Carl M. Hubbard, and Daniel T. Walz, professors of finance in the Department of Business Administration, Trinity University, San Antonio, Texas.

[3] *The Millionaire Next Door*, by Thomas J. Stanley and William D. Danko, Simon and Schuster, 1998

Chapter 7

[1] Thrift Savings Plan website at http://www.tsp.gov. A summary chart of expense ratios can be found at http://www.tsp.gov/rates/tsp-expense-ratio.pdf.

[2] *On War*, by General Carl von Clausewitz, The complete translation by Colonel J.J. Graham, published by N. Trübner, London, 1873. A copy is available online at http://www.clausewitz.com/readings/OnWar1873/TOC.htm

[3] The "Get-a-Life Tree" is found in *How to Retire Happy, Wild, and Free: Retirement Wisdom That You Won't Get from Your Financial Adviser*, by Ernie J. Zelinski, page 80 of the 2004 edition.

Chapter 8

[1] *Cashing in on the American Dream: How to Retire at 35*, by Paul Terhorst, 1988.

[2] The "Get-a-Life Tree" is found in *How to Retire Happy, Wild, and Free: Retirement Wisdom That You Won't Get from Your Financial Adviser*, by Ernie J. Zelinski, page 80 of the 2004 edition.

Appendix E

[1] http://www.tsp.gov/calc/annuity/calcAnnuityResults.cfm

[2] "The Value of Retirement Income Streams: The Value of Military Retirement," research paper by William W. Jennings and William Reichenstein, May 2001.

[3] "The High Cost of a No-Fee, No-Commission Single Premium Immediate Annuity (SPIA)," John P. Greaney, http://www.retireearlyhomepage.com/annuity_costs.html, July 2009.

Appendix F

[1] Tversky, A., and Kahneman, D. (1981). "Prospect Theory: An analysis of decision under risk," *Econometrica* Vol 47 (1979), pp. 263-91. Also "The framing of decisions and the psychology of choice," Science, 211, 453-458.

[2] Markowitz, Harry M. (1952). "Portfolio Selection," *Journal of Finance* 7 (1): 77–91.

[3] "Bank of America slides to quarterly loss," *Los Angeles Times,* January 17, 2009, http://articles.latimes.com/2009/jan/17/business/fi-bofa17.

[4] For example, the StayNavy retirement calculator at https://staynavytools.bol.navy.mil/RetCalc/Default.aspx.

[5] A $250,000 portfolio split 50/50 between stocks and bonds has $125,000 in each asset class. A $1 million pension value adds $1 million of bonds for a total of $1,250,000 split between $125,000 in stocks (10%) and $1,125,000 ($1 million + $125,000) in bonds (90%).

[6] Steve P. Fraser, William W. Jennings, David R. King, "Strategic asset allocation for individual investors: the impact of the present value of Social Security benefits," *Financial Services Review* 9 (2000), 295–326.

[7] Ralph Nelson, *The $avvy $ailor* and *The $avvy Officer*, published 2002.

BIBLIOGRAPHY

"Bank of America slides to quarterly loss." *Los Angeles Times.* 17 January 2009. 31 August 2009. http://articles.latimes.com/2009/jan/17/business/fi-bofa17.

Bernstein, William J. "The Retirement Calculator from Hell, Part III." *Efficient Frontier.* 2001. William J. Bernstein. 01 September 2009. http://www.efficientfrontier.com/ef/901/hell3.htm.

Brinson, Gary P., Brian D. Singer, and Gilbert L. Beebower. "Determinants of Portfolio Performance II: An Update." *Financial Analysts Journal* 47 (1991): 40-48. *CFA Institute Publications.* CFA Institute. 31 August 2009. http://www.cfapubs.org/doi/abs/10.2469/faj.v47.n3.40.

Clyatt, Bob. *Work Less, Live More: The New Way to Retire Early.* Berkeley, CA: Nolo, 2005.

"Comparing Options." *U.S. Department of Defense Official Website.* 01 September 2009. http://www.defenselink.mil/militarypay/retirement/ad/07_rc_comparingoptions.html.

Cooley, Philip L., Carl M. Hubbard, and Daniel T. Walz. "Retirement Savings: Choosing a Withdrawal Rate That Is Sustainable." *AAII Journal* XX (1998). 31 August 2009. http://bobsfiles.home.att.net/trinity.htm.

Dimson, Elroy, Paul Marsh, and Mike Staunton. *Triumph of the Optimists: 101 Years of Global Investment Returns.* New York: Princeton UP, 2002.

Fraser, Steve P., William W. Jennings, and David R. King. "Strategic Asset Allocation for Individual Investors: The Impact of the Present Value of Social Security Benefits." *Financial Services Review* 9 (2006). SSRN. 10 July 2006. Social Science Research Network. 31 August 2009. http://papers.ssrn.com/sol3/papers.cfm?abstract_id=912809.

Freedman, Marc. *Encore: Finding Work that Matters in the Second Half of Life.* New York: Public Affairs, 2008.

Freedman, Marc. *Prime Time: How Baby Boomers Will Revolutionize Retirement and Transform America.* New York: Public Affairs, 2002.

Gladwell, Malcolm. *The Story of Success*. New York: Little, Brown and Co., 2008.

Graves, Russ T. "A Comparative Study of the Life Satisfaction of Early Retirement Military Officers." Thesis, Texas A&M University, 2005. August 2005. 31 August 2009. http://txspace.tamu.edu/bitstream/handle/1969.1/2581/etd-tamu-2005B-EPSY-Graves.pdf?sequence=1.

Greaney, John P. "The High Cost of a No-Fee, No-Commission Single Premium Immediate Annuity (SPIA)." *The Retire Early Home Page.* 1 July 2009. 01 September 2009. http://www.retireearlyhomepage.com/annuity_costs.html.

Jennings, William W., and Reichenstein William. "The value of retirement income streams: the value of military retirement." *Financial Services Review* 10 (2001): 19-35.

Kaderli, Billy, and Akaisha Kaderli. *The Adventurer's Guide to Early Retirement. The Adventurer's Guide.* 2009. The Kaderlis' website. 31 August 2009. http://retireearlylifestyle.com/orderpage.htm.

Markowitz, Harry M. "Portfolio Selection." *Journal of Finance* 7 (1952): 77-91.

Milevsky, Moshe A. *Are You a Stock or a Bond? Using Your Unique Human Capital to Generate a Secure Financial Future*. Upper Saddle River, N.J: FT P, 2009.

"Military Retirement: One Chance to Get It Right." 1 Apr. 2008. USAA. 31 August 2009. https://content.usaa.com/mcontent/static_assets/Media/military_retirement_ebook_download.pdf?cacheid=390930281.

"The Military Retirement System (Part 2) – Military Benefits – Military.com." Military.com. 01 September 2009. http://www.military.com/benefits/military-pay/retired-pay/military-retirement-system-part-2.

Nelson, Ralph. *The $avvy Sailor (An Eye-Opening Guide To One Sailor's Personal Financial Saga!)*. Green Forest: Master Plan, Inc., 2002.

Philpott, Tom. "Redux Bonus: Bad Deal Gets Worse." Military.com. 31 August 2009. http://www.military.com/features/0,15240,173719,00.html?wh=benefits.

Philpott, Tom. "Redux Bonus Repeal Sought." Military.com. 31 August 2009. http://www.military.com/features/0,15240,185348,00.html.

Philpott, Tom. "Retired Pay Differences Rise." *Military Update* 27 March 2008. Military.com. 31 August 2009. http://www.military.com/features/0,15240,164817,00.html?wh=benefits.

Quester, Aline O., Lewis G. Lee, and Ian MacLeod. "The Retirement Choice." 07 April 2004. 31 August 2009. http://www.cna.org/documents/D0003713.A4.pdf.

Segal, David R., and Mady Wechsler Segal. "America's Military Population." *Population Bulletin* 59 (2004). Population Reference Bureau. 31 August 2009. http://www.prb.org/Source/ACF1396.pdf.

Stanley, Thomas J. *The Millionaire Next Door: The Surprising Secrets of America's Wealthy*. New York: Pocket Books, 1998.

"StayNAVY's Retirement Calculator." Department of the Navy. 31 August 2009. https://staynavytools.bol.navy.mil/RetCalc/Default.aspx.

Strobridge, Steve. "As I See It: REDUX Career Status Bonus A $30,000 Scandal." *MOAA – The Military Officers Association of America Web Base*. MOAA. 31 August 2009. http://www.moaa.org/lac/lac_asiseeit/lac_asiseeit_2009/lac_asiseeit_090219.htm.

Terhorst, Paul. *Cashing in on the American Dream: How to Retire at 35*. New York: Bantam, 1988.

"Thrift Savings Fund Expense Ratio." 2007. Thrift Savings Plan. 31 August 2009. http://www.tsp.gov/rates/tsp-expense-ratio.pdf.

"TSP: Annuity Calculator." *The Official TSP Home Page, maintained by FRTIB*. 22 May 2008. 01 September 2009. http://www.tsp.gov/index.shtml.

Tversky, A., and D. Kahneman. "Prospect Theory: An analysis of decision under risk." *Econometrica* 47 (1979): 263-91.

Tversky, A., and D. Kahneman. "The Framing of Decisions and the Psychology of Choice." *Science* 30 January 1981: 453-58. 31 August 2009. http://www-psych.stanford.edu/~knutson/bad/tversky81.pdf.

"Typical Solutions." *U.S. Department of Defense Official Website*. 01 September 2009. http://www.defenselink.mil/militarypay/retirement/ad/08_rc_typicalsituations.html.

Von Clausewitz, Carl. *On War by Carl Von Clausewitz*. Translated by Col. J.J. Graham. New York: Dorset Press, 1991.

Zelinski, Ernie J. *The Joy of Not Working: A Book for the Retired, Unemployed and Overworked*. Berkeley: Ten Speed Press, 2003.

Zelinski, Ernie J. *How to Retire Happy, Wild, and Free: Retirement Wisdom That You Won't Get from Your Financial Advisor*. New York: VIP Books, 2004.

RECOMMENDED READING

This list was compiled from the recommendations of dozens of veterans and their families. The author has personally read or used all of them and was not paid, compensated, or otherwise bribed to recommend them. Many of them are free through a website or local library. The products are all worth their price, but more value can be extracted by working through the free resources before spending money.

The website links may have changed since the date of publication, so please visit http://The-Military-Guide.com for the latest version of website references. The website includes this entire list as well as many more links to special topics like expatriate living and perpetual travel. Instead of reading through every word of this section, it may be easier to use the website and its links to go directly to the topics of your choice.

Military Books

Armed Forces Guide to Personal Financial Planning, Margaret Belknap and Michael Marty. One of the best decision-making guides for military issues.

The Military Advantage, Chris Michel of Military.com. Best benefits book.

The $avvy $ailor and *The $avvy Officer*, Ralph Nelson. Step-by-step explanations of avoiding debt, starting a savings system, and planning for a career of earnings and investments.

Retirement Books

Work Less, Live More, Bob Clyatt. The latest and best on early retirement and semi-retirement. Includes CD of spreadsheets and other analysis tools.

The Adventurer's Guide to Early Retirement, Billy and Akaisha Kaderli. The latest and best on perpetual travel. Download from www.Retire EarlyLifestyle.com.

Cashing in on the American Dream: How to Retire at 35, Paul Terhorst. One of the first early-retirement books. Timeless retirement lifestyle advice.

Get A Life: You Don't Need a Million to Retire Well, Ralph Warner. Retirement lifestyle advice from the co-founder of Nolo.

How To Retire Early and Live Well, Gillette Edmunds. Another classic manual.

Rags to Retirement, Alan Lavine. Extreme frugality, expatriate living, perpetual travel, and other creative ideas.

What Color is Your Parachute? For Retirement, John E. Nelson and Richard N. Bolles. Thorough advice on self-assessment and retirement lifestyle planning.

The Joy of Not Working and *How to Retire Happy, Wild, and Free*, Ernie Zelinski. "Get-a-Life Tree" and other planning tools.

Prime Time and *Encore,* Marc Freedman. "Bridge careers" and a lifetime of service.

Retiring as a Career: Making the Most of Your Retirement, Betsy Kyte Newman. Planning your retirement lifestyle and thinking through the issues.

Frugality and Saving Books

Your Money or Your Life, Joe Dominguez. The classic work that inspired the simple-living movement.

The Complete Tightwad Gazette, Amy Dacyczyn. Complete and detailed frugal advice from a veteran's spouse.

The Millionaire Next Door, Thomas Stanley and William Danko. The demographics and mindsets of millionaires applied to savings and business.

The Ultimate Cheapskate: Road Map to True Riches Jeff Yeager. "Focus on big lifestyle decisions, not the $3 cup of coffee."

Investing Books

The Intelligent Investor, Benjamin Graham. The bible of value investing since 1949. Multiple editions and updates.

The Four Pillars of Investing and *The Intelligent Asset Allocator*, William Bernstein. Asset allocation clearly explained with examples of real-life investment portfolios.

Triumph of the Optimists, Elroy Dimson, Paul Marsh, and Mike Staunton. Pragmatic review of over a century of investment returns among 16 countries.

Why Smart People Make Big Money Mistakes, Gary Belsky and Thomas Gilovich. Vital investor psychology guide for self-assessment.

The Retirement Savings Time Bomb and *Parlay Your IRA into a Family Fortune,* Ed Slott. How to fund, maintain, convert, and withdraw from IRAs.

Are You a Stock or a Bond?, Moshe Milevsky. Applies novel concept of "human capital" to investing and asset allocation.

A Random Walk Down Wall Street, Burton Malkiel. Classic analysis of efficient market hypothesis and index-fund investing.

All About Asset Allocation, Rick Ferri. Explains the basics of asset allocation and starting an investment portfolio.

The Only Guide to a Winning Investment Strategy You'll Ever Need, Larry Swedroe. Clear and basic advice on starting and maintaining an investment portfolio.

Stocks for the Long Run, Jeremy J. Siegel. Advocates benefits of buy-and-hold investing.

The Coffeehouse Investor, Bill Schultheis. Low-maintenance portfolios for the deployed (or lazy) investor.

The Bogleheads' Guide to Investing, Taylor Larimore, Mel Lindauer, and Michael LeBoeuf. Leading advocates of Bogle's invention of index-fund investing.

The Bogleheads' Guide to Retirement Planning, Taylor Larimore, Mel Lindauer, Richard Ferri, and Laura F. Dogu. Bogle's index-fund advocates on saving and spending during retirement.

Common Sense on Mutual Funds and *The Little Book of Common Sense Investing,* John Bogle. Founder of the first modern index fund and Vanguard.

J.K. Lasser's Your Winning Retirement Plan, Henry "Bud" Hebeler. Innovative and very conservative "negative feedback" approach to investment planning and adjusting retirement spending to investment returns. Extremely detailed analysis of when to take Social Security benefits.

The Informed Investor, Frank Armstrong III. A Vietnam veteran and financial adviser on common-sense investing.

Investing in Real Estate (6th edition), Andrew McLean and Gary W. Eldred. Common-sense and hype-free guide to analyzing and buying investment property.

"Landlording" (11th edition or later), Leigh Robinson *The best modern guide on managing rental real estate. Not for the lazy or faint of heart.*

Military Research Papers

A Comparative Study of the Life Satisfaction of Early Retirement Military Officers, doctoral dissertation, Russ T. Graves, professor at Texas A&M College, 2005. Available online at http://repositories.tdl.org/tdl/handle/1969.1/2581/etd-tamu-2005B-EPSY-Graves.pdf. Analysis of survey data indicating that the vast majority of officers immediately begin civilian careers after military retirement.

America's Military Population, David R. and Mady Wechsler Segal, excerpted from the December 2004 issue of the Population Reference Bureau's *Population Bulletin*, Vol 59, No 4. Available online at http://www.prb.org/Source/ACF1396.pdf. Eye-opening demographics and statistics on veterans and the services.

DoD Statistical Report on the Military Retirement System: http://www.defenselink.mil/actuary/statbook08.pdf. Detailed summary of military retirees age, rank, service, location, and other factors.

Financial Research Papers

Reprinted study of 4% safe withdrawal rate (www.fpanet.org/journal/articles/2004_Issues/jfp0304-art8.cfm): *Determining Withdrawal Rates Using Historical Data,* William P. Bengen, originally published in Journal of Financial Planning, vol. 7, no. 4 (October 1994), pp. 171-80. Reprinted with "Best Of" collection in 2004. First study to analyze withdrawal rates and conclude that 4% plus inflation was "safe."

The Trinity Study (http://bobsfiles.home.att.net/trinity.htm): *Retirement Savings: Choosing a Withdrawal Rate That is Sustainable*, Philip L. Cooley, Carl M. Hubbard, and Daniel T. Walz, professors of finance in the Department of Business Administration, Trinity University, San Antonio, Texas. Included in Scott Burns's column at http://www.dallasnews.com/sharedcontent/dws/bus/scottburns/readers/stories/SBportfoliosurvival.f5a90da.html. Widely publicized study confirming 4% safe withdrawal rate.

Asset allocation effect on portfolio (http://www.cfapubs.org/doi/pdf/10.2469/faj.v51.n1.1869): *Determinants of portfolio performance,* Gary Brinson, Randolf Hood, Gilbert Beebower. *Financial Analysis Journal,* July-August 1986, pp. 39-44. Limited data from pension funds supports importance of asset allocation in returns.

Tversky, A., and Kahneman, D. (1981). *Prospect Theory: An Analysis of Decision Under Risk,* Econometrica Vol 47 (1979), pp. 263-91. Also *The Framing of Decisions and the Psychology of Choice,* Science, 211, 453-458. Classic studies of investor psychology.

Jennings, William W., and Reichenstein,William. "The Value of Retirement Income Streams: The Value of Military Retirement," *Financial Services Review* 10 (2001): 19-35. The importance of considering retirement income when choosing an asset allocation.

Fraser, Steve P., William W. Jennings, and David R. King. *Strategic Asset Allocation for Individual Investors: The Impact of the Present Value of Social Security Benefits, Financial Services Review* 9 (2006). SSRN. 10 July 2006. Social Science Research Network. 31 Aug. 2009.http://papers.ssrn.com/sol3/papers.cfm?abstract_id=912809. Analyzes the significant impact of Social Security benefits on asset allocation.

Raddr's home page (http://raddr-pages.com/research/index.htm): An early retiree's analysis of asset allocation, diversification, and withdrawal rates.

Military Articles

Summary of the military retirement system (two parts): http://www.military.com/benefits/military-pay/retired-pay/military-retirement-system http://www.military.com/benefits/military-pay/retired-pay/military-retirement-system-part-2. Detailed explanation of military retirement systems and calculations.

USAA's *Military Retirement: One Chance to Get It Right* ebook (https://content.usaa.com/mcontent/static_assets/Media/military_retirement_ebook_download.pdf?cacheid=390930281), accessed from http://www.USAA.com/transition. Best summary of the military retirement system.

DoD analysis of REDUX: http://www.defenselink.mil/militarypay/retirement/ad/07_rc_comparingoptions.html. Official analysis of REDUX options

DoD summary of REDUX at specific ranks and years of service: http://
www.defenselink.mil/militarypay/retirement/ad/08_rc_typicalsituations.
html. Detailed analysis of REDUX retirement for various ranks and years of
service.

CNA Corporation REDUX study: http://www.cna.org/documents/D0003713.
A4.pdf. Detailed study of disadvantages and adverse impacts of REDUX
retirement system.

Military.com analysis of REDUX: http://www.military.com/benefits/military-
pay/retired-pay/military-retirement-system-part-2. Examples of adverse
impacts of REDUX retirement system.

Military Times, "REDUX Bonus: Bad Deal Gets Worse." http://www.
military.com/features/0,15240,173719,00.html?wh=benefits. Popular
summary of REDUX retirement issues and pitfalls.

Military Times, "REDUX Bonus Repeal Sought." http://www.military.
com/features/0,15240,185348,00.html. Summary of controversy surrounding
REDUX retirement system.

"As I See It," Military Officer's Association of America article on REDUX:
http://www.moaa.org/lac/lac_asiseeit/lac_asiseeit_2009/lac_asiseeit_090219.
htm. Military advocate's opinion of REDUX retirement system.

MOAA on Roth TSP proposal: http://www.moaa.org/lac/lac_asiseeit/lac_
asiseeit_2009/lac_asiseeit_090323.htm. Review of legislation and service
implementation of Roth Thrift Savings Plan.

MSN Money, "Does Military Service Still Pay?." http://articles.
moneycentral.msn.com/CollegeAndFamily/MoneyInYour20s/DoesMilitary
ServiceStillPay.aspx?page=all. Popular analysis of military pay scales versus
civilian careers.

Military Times, "Retired Pay Differences Rise." http://www.military.com/
features/0,15240,164817,00.html. Analysis of effectiveness of military
pension COLA at maintaining retiree's purchasing power.

Military Times, "Active Duty Retirees Die Sooner Than Reservists." http://
www.military.com/features/0,15240,183052,00.html. Statistical study of
military retiree mortality rates.

Kiplinger's, "Personal Finance for Military Families." http://www.kiplinger. com/money/military/pdfs/Military_Families_Final.pdf?kipad_id=65. Clear summary of financial considerations for veterans and their families.

Money Magazine, "Retired at 40: The Nielsens." http://money.cnn.com/ magazines/moneymag/moneymag_archive/2008/02/01/102902034/index. htm. Profile of a dual-military couple and their family and their retirement lifestyle.

Financial Articles

William Bernstein's "Retirement Calculator from Hell" five-part series:
>http://www.efficientfrontier.com/ef/998/hell.htm
>http://www.efficientfrontier.com/ef/101/hell101.htm
>http://www.efficientfrontier.com/ef/901/hell3.htm
>http://www.efficientfrontier.com/ef/103/hell4.htm
>http://www.efficientfrontier.com/ef/403/hell5.htm

Why retirement calculators can't guarantee 100% success.

Newsletters on the retirement transition: http://www.MyNextPhase.com/ newsletter. "Tough love" approach to retirement lifestyle issues.

Philip Greenspun on early retirement: http://philip.greenspun.com/ materialism/early-retirement/. Practical advice on getting things done before and during retirement.

"Six myths of Social Security." http://investopedia.com/printable.asp?a=/ articles/retirement/08/6-retirement-myths.asp. Review of Social Security funding and legislation issues.

"Is the Safe Withdrawal Rate Sometimes Too Safe?." http://www.kitces. com/assets/pdfs/Kitces_Report_May_2008.pdf. Excessively conservative withdrawal rates can reduce quality of retirement life.

Military Websites

www.Military.com

DoD's REDUX website: http://www.defenselink.mil/militarypay/retirement/ad/07_rc_comparingoptions.html StayNavy retirement pay calculator: https://staynavytools.bol.navy.mil/RetCalc/Default.aspx Computing retired military pay: http://www.military.com/benefits/military-pay/retired-pay/computing-retired-military-pay?ESRC=retirees.nl.

USAA's "Military Retirement" summary: https://www.usaa.com/inet/ent_utils/McStaticPages?key=ret_understand_your_military_retirement.

DFAS pay tables: http://www.dfas.mil/militarypay/militarypaytables.html.

TSP FAQs: http://www.tsp.gov/uniserv/features/index.html.

TSP annuity calculator: http://www.tsp.gov/calc/annuity/annuity.cfm.

Military Handbooks: http://www.militaryhandbooks.com/.

Together We Served Navy and its other service websites: http://navy.togetherweserved.com.

Retirement Websites

www.Early-Retirement.org. The biggest and busiest of the bunch with over 8,000 members, over seven years, and more than 500,000 posts.

Retire Early home page (http://www.retireearlyhomepage.com): Over a decade of research, articles, and reviews by an early retirement pioneer.

Bogleheads (http://www.bogleheads.org): Followers of John Bogle's index investing.

Bob Clyatt's *Work Less, Live More*: http://www.workless-livemore.com.

Billy and Akaisha Kaderli: http://www.retireearlylifestyle.com. Tireless perpetual travelers with an online early-retirement guide.

Paul and Vicki Terhorst: http://sites.google.com/site/paulvicgroup/. Trailblazing early retirees and perpetual travelers.

The Efficient Frontier (http://www.efficientfrontier.com): Research on asset allocation and estimating safe withdrawal rates.

The Dollar $tretcher (http://www.stretcher.com): *O*ne of the best websites about saving, paying off debt, and living with money. Many more links to www.Bankrate.com.

Gummy's Stuff (http://www.gummy-stuff.org): Absolute treasure trove of financial information, explanations, and entertainment. Retired professor Peter Ponzo is no longer updating the site, but a cache is available at http://74.125.155.132/search?q=cache:SeduywLrSPgJ:www.gummy-stuff. org/+gummy+stuff+excel&cd=2&hl=en&ct=clnk&gl=us.

FundAlarm (http://www.fundalarm.com/wwwboard/wwwboard.html): Revealing, irreverent, and occasionally ruthless critiques of the mutual-fund industry.

SimpleLiving.net (http://www.simpleliving.net): The triumphs and details of frugal living and simple lifestyles.

Ed Slott's IRA Help discussion board (http://www.irahelp.com/forum/):Best discussion board for questions about IRAs, no matter how obscure or complex.

Fairmark (http://www.fairmark.com/index.htm): Extremely comprehensive tax guide.

Your Money or Your Life updates (www.yourmoneyoryourlife.org): Vicki Robin continues Joe Dominguez's work.

Bud Hebeler's "Analyze Now!" retirement research (http://www.analyzenow. com): Innovative and very conservative "negative feedback" approach to varying retirement spending with investment returns. Extremely detailed analysis of when to take Social Security benefits.

Early Retirement Extreme (http://earlyretirementextreme.com): Very early retiree with unusual ideas on frugality and on achieving ER in just a few years. Not for the faint of heart, but many valuable concepts to choose from.

Bogleheads reference library (http://www.bogleheads.org/forum/viewtopic. php?t=5954 and http://www.bogleheads.org/readbooks.htm): Many more resources on low-cost investing and index funds.

"My Next Phase" (http://www.mynextphase.com): Retirement surveys and counseling for adjusting retirement plans to personality, temperament, and interests. Valuable advice, but the "tough love" approach seems a little extreme. See the link to their newsletters in the *Financial Articles* section.

Bureau of Labor and Statistics (http://www.bls.gov/data/inflation_calculator. htm): *What was a dollar worth back then?* inflation calculator. Details on the Consumer Price Index, the Producer Price Index, and the Employment Cost Index.

www.Investopedia.com: Huge encyclopedia of investment terms and concepts.

Retirement Calculators and Tools

FIRECalc (http://www.fireseeker.com): The latest free version of the original early-retirement calculator, with different planning options for different scenarios.

FinancialEngines (http://www.financialengines.com): Free trial of extremely detailed retirement calculator. Allows changing many more parameters than a typical retirement calculator.

"Analyze Now!" (http://www.analyzenow.com/Free%20Programs/free_ programs.htm): Spreadsheets and programs for analyzing different retirement scenarios from "Bud" Hebeler's retirement planner.

ESPlanner (http://www.esplanner.com): Retirement planning software designed to level out spending and consumption over the span of a retirement. Extremely detailed data entry for those who want to investigate all parameters and intricacies of retirement financial planning.

Optimal Retirement Planner (http://www.i-orp.com): Maximizes after-tax retirement spending by optimizing the timing of retirement account withdrawals, including Social Security benefits.

Day clocks (http://www.dayclocks.com): This is not a joke! Read Chapter 8 about a retiree's typical day.

The Author

Doug Nordman retired at the age of 41 after 20 years with the U.S. Navy's submarine force. He's an enthusiastic surfer, an omnivorous reader, a martial arts student, and a veteran of many chaotic home-improvement projects. After eight years of early retirement he's an expert at answering the question "But what do you DO all day?" He and his spouse, a retired Navy Reservist, are raising a teenager in Hawaii. Life is busier than ever and they can't imagine where they found the time to go to work.

INDEX

ORDER FORM

THE FOLLOWING resources are available directly from Impact Publications. Full descriptions of each title, some of which are referenced throughout this book, as well as downloadable catalogs and related products can be found at www.impactpublications.com. Complete this form or list the titles, include shipping (see formula at the end), enclose payment, and send your order to:

IMPACT PUBLICATIONS
9104 Manassas Drive, Suite N
Manassas Park, VA 20111-5211 USA
1-800-361-1055 (orders only)
Tel. 703-361-7300 or Fax 703-335-9486
Email address: query@impactpublications.com
Quick & easy online ordering: www.impactpublications.com

Orders from individuals must be prepaid by check, money order, or major credit card. We accept telephone, fax, and email orders.

Qty.	Titles	Price	TOTAL
Military Benefits, Education, Law, and VA Claims			
____	The Military Advantage (annual)	$ 26.95	_____
____	Claims Denied: How to Appeal a VA Denial	16.95	_____
____	Complete Idiot's Guide to Your Military and Veterans Benefits	18.95	_____
____	Servicemember's Guide to a College Degree	14.95	_____
____	Servicemember's Legal Guide	19.95	_____
____	Veterans Benefits for Dummies	19.99	_____
____	Veteran's Guide to Benefits	16.95	_____
____	The Veteran's PTSD Handbook: How to File and Collect on Claims	19.95	_____
____	Veteran's Survival Guide: How to File and Collect on VA Claims	17.95	_____
Retirement			
____	50 Fabulous Places to Retire in America	24.95	_____
____	The AARP Retirement Survival Guide	14.95	_____
____	America's 100 Best Places to Retire	18.95	_____
____	The Bogleheads' Guide to Retirement Planning	14.95	_____
____	Encore: Finding Work That Matters in the Second Half of Life	16.95	_____
____	Get a Life: You Don't Need a Million to Retire Well	24.99	_____

Qty.	Titles	Price	TOTAL
____	How to Love Your Retirement	16.95	_____
____	How to Retire Happy	18.95	_____
____	How to Retire Happy, Wild, and Free	16.95	_____
____	The Joy of Not Working	16.99	_____
____	The New Retirement	19.95	_____
____	The New Rules of Retirement	26.95	_____
____	Quit Your Job and Grow Some Hair	15.95	_____
____	Retirement Planning Kit (39 books)	684.95	_____
____	Rich Dad's Retire Young Retire Rich	17.95	_____
____	Save Your Retirement	14.99	_____
____	The Smartest Retirement Book You'll Ever Read	21.95	_____
____	Stop Sitting on Your Assets	22.95	_____
____	Super-Charged Retirement	16.95	_____
____	What Color Is Your Parachute? For Retirement	16.99	_____
____	Work Less, Live More	17.99	_____

Investing

Qty.	Titles	Price	TOTAL
____	All About Asset Allocation	21.95	_____
____	Are You a Stock or a Bond? Create Your Own Pension Plan for a Secure Financial Future	27.99	_____
____	The Bogleheads' Guide to Investing	18.95	_____
____	Common Sense on Mutual Funds	29.95	_____
____	The Four Pillars of Investing: Lessons for Building a Winning Portfolio	30.00	_____
____	The Informed Investor	17.95	_____
____	The Intelligent Asset Allocator: How to Build Your Portfolio to Maximize Returns and Minimize Risk	22.95	_____
____	Investing Demystified	22.95	_____
____	Investing in Real Estate	19.95	_____
____	Landlording	29.95	_____
____	The Little Book of Common Sense Investing	19.95	_____
____	Military Savings, Investing, and Frugality Kit	599.95	_____
____	The New Coffeehouse Investor	22.95	_____
____	Parlay Your IRA Into a Family Fortune	16.00	_____
____	A Random Walk Down Wall Street: The Time-Tested Strategy for Successful Investing	29.95	_____
____	The Retirement Savings Time Bomb	17.00	_____
____	Stocks for the Long Run	34.95	_____
____	Why Smart People Make Big Money Mistakes	15.00	_____

Qty.	Titles	Price	TOTAL

Savings and Frugality

____	The Armed Forces Guide to Personal Financial Planning	22.95	_____
____	Lighten Up: Love What You Have, Have What You Need	26.00	_____
____	The Millionaire Next Door	16.95	_____
____	The Money Book for the Young, Fabulous, and Broke	16.00	_____
____	The Money Class	26.00	_____
____	Financial Planning Demystified	14.95	_____
____	Smart and Simple Financial Strategies for Busy People	26.00	_____
____	Total Money Makeover	24.99	_____
____	The Truth About Money	19.99	_____
____	The Ultimate Cheapskate's Road Map to True Riches	12.95	_____
____	Your Money or Your Life: 9 Steps to Transforming Your Relationship With Money and Achieving Financial Independence	16.00	_____

Attitude, Motivation, and Success

____	Attitude Is Everything	16.99	_____
____	Awaken the Giant Within	16.95	_____
____	Create Your Own Future	18.95	_____
____	Finding Your Own North Star	15.00	_____
____	Goals! How to Get Everything Faster Than You Thought Possible	18.95	_____
____	Outliers: The Story of Success	27.99	_____
____	The Success Principles	17.99	_____

Military Finances, Spouses, and Families

____	Armed Forces Guide to Personal Financial Planning	22.95	_____
____	Chicken Soup for the Military Wife's Soul	14.95	_____
____	Chicken Soup for the Veteran's Soul	14.95	_____
____	Complete Idiot's Guide to Life as a Military Spouse	12.95	_____
____	Complete Idiot's Guide to Military Veteran's Benefits	18.95	_____
____	A Family's Guide to the Military for Dummies	19.99	_____
____	Military Spouse Finance Guide	19.95	_____
____	Military Spouse's Complete Guide to Career Success	17.95	_____
____	Today's Military Wife	19.95	_____

Qty.	Titles	Price	TOTAL

Pocket Guides

____	Military Family Benefits Pocket Guide	2.95	_____
____	Military Family Education Pocket Guide	2.95	_____
____	Military Family Legal Pocket Guide	2.95	_____
____	Military Family Recreation and Travel Pocket Guide	2.95	_____
____	Military Financial Independence & Retirement	2.95	_____
____	Military Personal Finance Pocket Guide	2.95	_____
____	Military Spouse's Employment Pocket Guide	2.95	_____
____	Military Spouse's Map Through the Maze	2.95	_____
____	Military-to-Civilian Transition Pocket Guide	2.95	_____
____	Military to Federal Government Employment	2.95	_____
____	The Quick Job Finding Pocket Guide	2.95	_____
____	Veteran's Business Start-Up Pocket Guide	2.95	_____
____	Top Military-Friendly Employers Pocket Guide	2.95	_____

Military Career Transition

____	Expert Resumes for Military-to-Civilian Transition	16.95	_____
____	Job Search: Marketing Your Military Experience	19.95	_____
____	Marketing Yourself for a Second Career DVD	49.95	_____
____	Military-to-Civilian Resumes and Letters	21.95	_____
____	Military-to-Civilian Transition Guide (annual)	9.95	_____
____	Military Transition to Civilian Success	21.95	_____

Job Loss and 30/30 Solutions

____	50 Jobs in 50 States	15.95	_____
____	The Difference	14.00	_____
____	Eliminated! Now What?	14.95	_____
____	Getting Back to Work	15.95	_____
____	Make Job Loss Work for You	12.95	_____
____	Quick 30/30 Job Solution	14.95	_____
____	Rebound	17.99	_____
____	Surviving a Layoff	9.95	_____

Career Exploration and Alternative Jobs

____	50 Best Jobs for Your Personality	17.95	_____
____	100 Fastest Growing Careers	17.95	_____
____	150 Best Recession-Proof Jobs	16.95	_____
____	150 Great Tech Prep Careers	29.95	_____
____	200 Best Jobs for College Graduates	16.95	_____
____	200 Best Jobs for Renewing America	17.95	_____

Qty.	Titles	Price	TOTAL
____	200 Best Jobs Through Apprenticeships	24.95	_____
____	250 Best-Paying Jobs	17.95	_____
____	300 Best Jobs Without a Four-Year Degree	17.95	_____
____	Best Career and Education Web Sites	14.95	_____
____	Best Jobs for the 21st Century	19.95	_____
____	Career Opportunities in the Food and Beverage Industry	18.95	_____
____	Career Opportunities in the Film Industry	18.95	_____
____	Career Opportunities in Library and Information Science	18.95	_____
____	Career Opportunities in the Music Industry	18.95	_____
____	Career Opportunities in the Publishing Industry	18.95	_____
____	Career Opportunities in Real Estate	18.95	_____
____	Career Opportunities in the Retail and Wholesale Industry	18.95	_____
____	Career Opportunities in the Sports Industry	18.95	_____
____	Career Opportunities in Travel and Hospitality	18.95	_____
____	Enhanced Occupational Outlook Handbook	39.95	_____
____	EZ Occupational Outlook Handbook	20.95	_____
____	Getting the Job You Really Wants	21.95	_____
____	Green Careers for Dummies	19.99	_____
____	Occupational Outlook Handbook	19.95	_____
____	Overnight Career Choice	9.95	_____
____	Progressive Careers	229.95	_____
____	The Sequel	12.95	_____
____	The Top 100: The Fastest Growing Careers for the 21st Century	19.95	_____
____	Top 100 Careers Without a Four-Year Degree	17.95	_____
____	Top 100 Health Care Careers	25.95	_____
____	Top 300 Careers	19.95	_____
____	Where the Jobs Are Now	18.95	_____
____	Young Person's Occupational Outlook Handbook	19.95	_____

Job Search and Career Planning

Qty.	Titles	Price	TOTAL
____	12 Steps to a New Career	16.99	_____
____	101 Best Ways to Land a Job in Troubled Times	14.95	_____
____	2011 Career Plan	9.95	_____
____	Coach Yourself to a New Career	18.95	_____
____	Get Hired in a Tough Market	16.95	_____
____	Get the Job You Want, Even When No One's Hiring	19.95	_____

Qty.	Titles	Price	TOTAL
____	Goals!	18.95	_____
____	Guerrilla Marketing for Job Hunters 2.0	21.95	_____
____	Job Hunter's Survival Guide	9.99	_____
____	Job Hunting Tips for People With Hot and Not-So-Hot Backgrounds	17.95	_____
____	Job Search Handbook for People With Disabilities	22.95	_____
____	Knock 'em Dead	15.95	_____
____	Quick Job Finding Pocket Guide (packet of 10)	23.60	_____
____	Quick Job Search (packet of 10)	44.95	_____
____	Self-Promotion for Introverts	18.95	_____
____	Smart New Way to Get Hired	14.95	_____
____	Strategies for Successful Career Change	16.99	_____
____	Your $100,000 Career Plan	14.95	_____
____	What Color Is Your Parachute?	18.99	_____
____	What Color Is Your Parachute? For Teens?	15.99	_____
____	What Color Is Your Parachute? For Retirement?	16.99	_____

Government and Nonprofit Jobs

Qty.	Titles	Price	TOTAL
____	Book of U.S. Government Jobs	26.95	_____
____	FBI Careers	19.95	_____
____	Guide to America's Federal Jobs	19.95	_____
____	Insider's Guide to the Peace Corps	14.95	_____
____	Jobs That Matter: Find a Stable, Fulfilling Career in Public Service	14.95	_____
____	Ten Steps to a Federal Job	28.95	_____

Resumes and Cover Letters

Qty.	Titles	Price	TOTAL
____	15-Minute Cover Letter	9.95	_____
____	101 Great Resumes	12.99	_____
____	Amazing Resumes	12.95	_____
____	Cover Letter Magic	18.95	_____
____	Cover Letters for Dummies	16.99	_____
____	Creating Your High School Portfolio	14.95	_____
____	Creating Your High School Resume	14.95	_____
____	Expert Resumes for Career Changers	16.95	_____
____	Expert Resumes for Computer and Web Jobs	17.95	_____
____	Expert Resumes for Health Care Careers	16.95	_____
____	Expert Resumes for Military-to-Civilian Transitions	16.95	_____
____	Fearless Resumes	12.95	_____
____	Federal Resume Guidebook	21.95	_____
____	Gallery of Best Resumes for People Without a Four-Year Degree	18.95	_____

Qty.	Titles	Price	TOTAL
____	Knock 'em Dead Cover Letters	12.95	_____
____	Knock 'em Dead Resumes	12.95	_____
____	The Quick Resume and Cover Letter Book	14.95	_____
____	Quick Resume Guide (packet of 10)	44.95	_____
____	Resumes for Dummies	16.99	_____
____	Resume Magic	18.95	_____
____	Sales and Marketing Resumes for 100,000 Careers	19.95	_____
____	Step-by-Step Cover Letters	19.95	_____
____	Step-by-Step Resumes	19.95	_____

Networking and New Media

Qty.	Titles	Price	TOTAL
____	Find a Job Through Social Networking	14.95	_____
____	How to Find a Job on LinkedIn, Facebook, Twitter, MySpace, and Other Social Networks	18.95	_____
____	Networking Survival Guide	16.95	_____
____	Networking for People Who Hate Networking	16.95	_____
____	Perfect Phrases for Professional Networking	10.95	_____
____	Twitter Job Search Guide	14.95	_____

Etiquette and Body Language

Qty.	Titles	Price	TOTAL
____	Body Language Handbook	15.99	_____
____	Don't Take the Last Donut	14.99	_____
____	Louder Than Words	24.99	_____
____	Winning Body Language	18.95	_____

Interviews and Salary Negotiations

Qty.	Titles	Price	TOTAL
____	101 Great Answers to the Toughest Interview Questions	12.99	_____
____	101 Smart Questions to Ask On Your Interview	12.99	_____
____	301 Best Questions to Ask On Your Interview	14.95	_____
____	Best Answers to the 201 Most Frequently Asked Interview Questions	14.95	_____
____	Can I Wear My Nose Ring to the Interview?	13.95	_____
____	Everything Practice Interview Book	14.95	_____
____	Get More Money on Your Next Job... in Any Economy	14.95	_____
____	Instant Interviews	16.95	_____
____	Job Interview Phrase Book	10.95	_____
____	Tell Me About Yourself	14.95	_____

Qty.	Titles	Price	TOTAL
____	Use Your Head to Get Your Foot in the Door	25.95	_____
____	Winning Job Interviews	12.99	_____

Entrepreneurship

Qty.	Titles	Price	TOTAL
____	The 9-to-5 Cure	14.95	_____
____	How to Make It Big As a Consultant	18.95	_____
____	Start Your Own Blogging Business	17.95	_____
____	Start Your Own Business and Hire Yourself	14.95	_____
____	Start Your Own Cleaning Business	17.95	_____
____	Start Your Own Consulting Business	17.95	_____
____	Start Your Own Import/Export Business	17.95	_____
____	Start Your Own Senior Services Business	17.95	_____

SUBTOTAL
Virginia residents add 5% sales tax _____

POSTAGE/HANDLING $5.00
($5 for first product and 9% of SUBTOTAL) _____

9% of SUBTOTAL

(Include an additional 15% if shipping
outside the continental United States) _____

TOTAL ENCLOSED _____

SHIP TO:

Name: _____

Address: _____

_____

_____

PAYMENT METHOD:

☐ I enclose check/money order for $ _____ made payable to
   IMPACT PUBLICATIONS.

☐ Please charge $ _____ to my credit card:

☐ Visa   ☐ MasterCard   ☐ American Express   ☐ Discover

Card # _____ Expiration date: ____/____

Signature _____

The Military
Savings, Investing,
and Frugality Kit

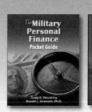

Whether you're still on active duty or dealing with transition and retirement issues, managing your financial future should be an important concern to you and your family. Here's the perfect collection of resources for achieving greater financial independence and personal freedom. Includes some of the best books on investing, savings, and living a more simple, goal-oriented life. Can purchase separately. **SPECIAL: $599.95 for all 30 books.**

INVESTING

- *All About Asset Allocation ($21.95)*
- *Are You a Stock or a Bond? Create Your Own Pension Plan for a Secure Financial Future ($27.99)*
- *The Bogleheads' Guide to Investing ($18.95)*
- *Common Sense on Mutual Funds ($29.95)*
- *The Four Pillars of Investing: Lessons for Building a Winning Portfolio ($30.00)*
- *The Informed Investor ($17.95)*
- *Investing in Real Estate ($19.95)*
- *The Little Book of Common Sense Investing ($19.95)*
- *The Military Financial Independence and Retirement Pocket Guide ($2.95)*
- *The Military Guide to Financial Independence and Retirement ($17.95)*
- *The New Coffeehouse Investor ($22.95)*
- *Parlay Your IRA Into a Family Fortune ($16.00)*
- *A Random Walk Down Wall Street ($29.95)*
- *The Retirement Savings Time Bomb ($17.00)*
- *Stocks for the Long Run ($34.95)*
- *Why Smart People Make Big Money Mistakes ($15.00)*

SMART MONEY MANAGEMENT

- *The 10 Commandments of Money ($25.95)*
- *Armed Forces Guide to Personal Financial Planning ($22.95)*
- *Debt Free for Life ($19.99)*
- *Lighten Up: Love What You Have, Have What You Need ($26.00)*
- *The Military Personal Finance Pocket Guide ($2.95)*
- *The Millionaire Next Door ($16.95)*
- *The Money Book for the Young, Fabulous, and Broke ($16.00)*
- *The Money Class ($26.00)*
- *Smart and Simple Financial Strategies for Busy People ($26.00)*
- *Smart is the New Rich ($24.95)*
- *Total Money Makeover ($24.99)*
- *The Truth About Money ($19.99)*
- *The Ultimate Cheapskate's Road Map to True Riches ($12.95)*
- *Your Money or Your Life ($16.00)*

ORDERS AND QUANTITY DISCOUNTS:
1-800-361-1055 or www.impactpublications.com

Powerful Pocket Guides for Military Success

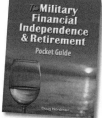
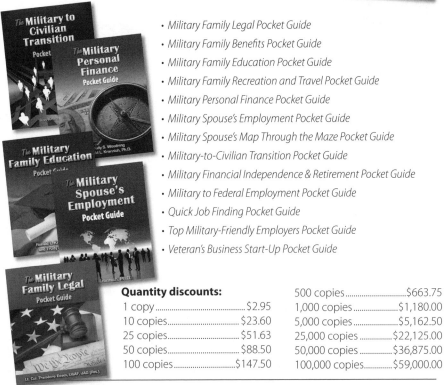

Military-to-Civilian Employment

Whether you're looking for a new career, a bridge job, or part-time employment, here are the key resources for assisting transitioning servicemembers and their families with finding jobs in the civilian world. Written and produced by leading military career transition specialists, these books and DVD are jam-packed with sound advice on organizing an effective job search campaign, obtaining transition assistance, assessing skills, setting goals, conducting research, networking, writing resumes and letters, dressing for success, interviewing for jobs, negotiating salaries, finding a government job, starting a business, understanding military benefits and retirement, implementing your plan, and much more. See page 197 for order information or visit Impact's online bookstore: www.impactpublications.com.

- *Military Financial Independence and Retirement Pocket Guide* ($2.95)
- *Military-to-Civilian Transition Guide* ($9.95)
- *Military-to-Civilian Transition Pocket Guide* ($2.95)
- *Military-to-Civilian Resumes and Letters* ($21.95)
- *Military-to-Federal Employment Pocket Guide* ($2.95)
- *Military Transition to Civilian Success* ($21.95)
- *Military Spouse's Complete Guide to Career Success* ($17.95)
- *Marketing Yourself for a Second Career DVD* ($49.95)
- *Top Military-Friendly Employers Pocket Guide* ($2.95)

ORDERS AND QUANTITY DISCOUNTS:
1-800-361-1055 or www.impactpublications.com

Career Transition Websites
Resources that Change Lives!

When it comes to providing assistance to transitional military personnel and their families, Impact has it all! Visit our websites that offer a wealth of information on finding jobs, changing careers, starting a business, managing families, parenting, acquiring education and training, retiring, traveling, investing, dealing with life's many ups and downs, and much more. We offer a rich collection of resources – books, DVDs, software, pamphlets, instruments, games, posters, audiobooks, curriculum packages, and special value kits. When it's time to look for useful life-changing resources, be sure to visit Impact for the latest in cutting-edge resources. We also operate a separate website the helps ex-offenders and their families, including incarcerated veterans, deal with critical re-entry and employment issues: www.exoffenderreentry.com.

ORDERS AND QUANTITY DISCOUNTS:
1-800-361-1055 or www.impactpublications.com